Touring Washington and Oregon Hot Springs

Help Us Keep This Guide Up to Date

Every effort has been made by the author and editors to make this guide as accurate and useful as possible. However, many things can change after a guide is published—trails are rerouted, regulations change, techniques evolve, facilities come under new management, etc.

We would love to hear from you concerning your experiences with this guide and how you feel it could be improved and kept up to date. While we may not be able to respond to all comments and suggestions, we'll take them to heart, and we'll also make certain to share them with the author. Please send your comments and suggestions to the following address:

The Globe Pequot Press
Reader Response/Editorial Department
P.O. Box 480
Guilford, CT 06437

Or you may e-mail us at:

editorial@globe-pequot.com

Thanks for your input, and happy travels!

Touring Washington and Oregon Hot Springs

Jeff Birkby

FALCON ®

GUILFORD, CONNECTICUT
HELENA, MONTANA
AN IMPRINT OF THE GLOBE PEQUOT PRESS

AFALCONGUIDE®

Text design: Amy Bransfield

Text photos: Jeff Birkby, unless otherwise noted

Maps: Topaz Maps Inc., © The Globe Pequot Press

Library of Congress Cataloguing-in-Publication Data is available.

ISBN 0-7627-1133-7

Manufactured in the United States of America

First Edition/First Printing

It would not be transcending the truth to state that all diseases are cured or largely benefited by the wonderful energy of these waters... health waits for those who may come and partake of this—life's elixir.

—Michael Earles, Sol Duc Hot Springs Resort, 1912

Contents

Acknowledgments

Many of the quirky histories of Washington and Oregon hot springs would never have found their way into this book without the help of dozens of librarians, Forest Service and Bureau of Land Management personnel, museum archivists, and hot spring resort owners. My thanks to all the public servants and private hot spring owners who searched their memories and file cabinets to unearth the quotes and facts that fill these pages.

Thanks also to my many friends and family members who turned what might have been lonely solo trips into joyful group adventures to Sol Duc, Breitenbush, Soap Lake, Scenic, and several other soaking spots during my two summers of research.

A final note of thanks to my brother Bob Birkby, who took his sharpened pen and critical eye to the early drafts of this book and who joined me on a memorable road trip to the steaming hot tubs at Doe Bay Resort on Orcas Island.

Map Legend

☼	Hot spring	🅰	Picnic area
———————	Roads	🅿	Parking area
= = = =	Unimproved road	▲	Campground
▬▬▬▬	Route to hot spring	⑂	Waterfall
- - - - - -	Hiking trail	‿	Mountain pass
— — —	National Forest boundary	▲	Summit
∿∿∿	Stream	🚶	Trailhead
⬭	Lake	⋈	Bridge
		▮	Ranger Station/ Headquarters/ Visitor Center

Locator Map
Washington and Oregon Hot Springs

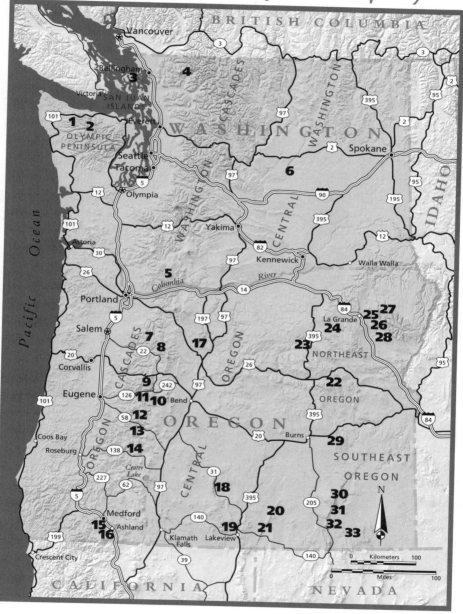

Introduction

Ask a dozen people on the streets of Portland or Seattle if they've ever been to one of Washington or Oregon's hot springs, and you'll be lucky if you find a single person who can even name one of the region's thermal wonders, let alone one who has soaked there. Most residents of the Pacific Northwest know of the volcanoes that form the Cascade Range—Mount Rainier, Mount Baker, Mount Hood, Mount St. Helens, and several others. Few realize, however, that the geologic forces that created the region's volcanoes also left behind dozens of actively bubbling reminders of the tremendous thermal energy that underlies the two states.

The hot springs of Washington and Oregon are as varied as the region's topography. Although many hot springs are sprinkled throughout the Cascade Range, quite a few thermal soaks are also found in the rolling Blue Mountains of Northeast Oregon, the dry southeastern Oregon deserts near the Nevada border, and the rain-drenched valleys of Washington's Olympic Peninsula.

Native American tribes in Washington and Oregon share legends of visiting the hot springs for curing their ills, and most hot springs were viewed as neutral territories where warring tribes could meet in peace to share the hot waters. Early pioneers reported seeing Native Americans building sauna huts on the shores of Soap Lake in central Washington and pouring mineral water from the lake onto heated rocks to create steam in the huts. Native Americans living on what is now the Warm Springs Reservation in north-central Oregon have bathed in local thermal waters for generations.

Hot springs offer a variety of options for a quick getaway.

Hot springs are reminders of the tremendous thermal energy beneath the earth's crust.

The first Europeans to see hot springs in Oregon and Washington were probably members of the Astor Expedition, who passed by the bubbling springs at Hot Lake in northeastern Oregon in 1812. Writer Washington Irving later retold these explorers' discovery of the region's first hot springs:

> Emerging from the chain of Blue Mountains, they descended upon a vast plain, almost a dead level, sixty miles in circumference, of excellent soil, with fine streams meandering through it in every direction, their courses marked out in the wide landscape by serpentine lines of cotton-wood trees, and willows, which fringed their banks, and afforded sustenance to great numbers of beavers and otters.
>
> In traversing this plain, they passed, close to the skirts of the hills, a great pool of water, three hundred yards in circumference, fed by a sulphur spring, about ten feet in diameter, boiling up in one corner. The vapor from this pool was extremely noisome, and tainted the air for a considerable distance. The place was much frequented by elk, which were found in considerable numbers in the adjacent mountains, and their horns, shed in the spring-time, were strewed in every direction around the pond.

By the 1840s thousands of settlers traveling west on the Oregon Trail had stopped at Hot Lake to rest and refresh themselves in the thermal water.

Most of the hot springs in Oregon and Washington had been discovered by the 1880s, and rustic bathhouses had been constructed at several. The peak of the region's hot spring popularity occurred during the first three decades of the twentieth century, when sumptuous resorts and sanitariums were constructed at hot springs throughout the region. Destination resorts built during this period included majestic Sol Duc Hot Springs Hotel on the Olympic Peninsula, the McCredie Springs Hotel in Oregon's Cascade Range, several hot spring resorts near Ashland in southwestern Oregon, and the resort hotels on the shores of central Washington's Soap Lake.

The austerity imposed by World War II, the trend toward modern medical treatments, and several devastating fires led to the decline of Oregon and Washington's most famous resorts. Several of the elegant resort hotels had disappeared by the 1950s, with some, such as McCredie and Olympic Hot Springs, reverting to natural hot spring pools with no visible signs of their glorious resort past. Some of the old resorts now lie abandoned, surrounded by weeds and NO TRESPASSING signs, like the historic Hot Lake Hotel near La Grande in northeastern Oregon. A few of the original resorts from the early 1900s are still in operation, including the historic Hotel St. Martin at Carson Hot Springs in the Columbia River Gorge, the Ritter Springs Hotel near the John Day River in northeastern Oregon, and the corrugated-steel bathhouse at Summer Lake Hot Springs north of Lakeview, Oregon.

Since the 1970s there has been a resurgence of interest in the hot springs of Washington and Oregon, as city dwellers have increasingly sought escape from the pressures of urban life. New resorts built in the past thirty years include the Kah-Nee-Ta Resort on the Warm Springs Reservation, the Lithia Springs Inn near Ashland, and the rebuilt lodge and pools at Sol Duc Hot Springs on the Olympic Peninsula.

Oregon and Washington hot springs offer all sorts of options for a quick getaway, including isolated soaking pools miles from civilization, family resorts crowded with weekend visitors from Seattle and Portland, holistic health centers deep in old-growth forests, and romantic inns with natural mineral-water hot tubs in cozy private rooms.

How to Use This Guide

Book Organization

Washington and Oregon offer an amazing variety of hot springs, as well as a number of ways to appreciate these thermal wonders. This book was written as a touring guide, focusing on both commercially developed and wilderness hot springs in Oregon and Washington that are easily accessible and that usually require no more than a short walk from your car to reach. Fortunately this requirement excludes only a handful of remote wilderness hot springs that take more intensive hikes or rafting to access.

A few of the hot springs described in this book are to be visited simply to savor their historical past, as they are currently off-limits for soaking. Others are quiet, primitive pools, where you can soak in solitude in a forested mountain valley or on an endless sagebrush prairie. Still other hot springs are found in quirky old resorts that look much the same as they did when they were built a century ago.

In some cases this guide does include descriptions of closed hot springs that have a compelling history and public access to vantage points. Medical Springs and Hot Lake Hotel near La Grande and Crump Geyser near Lakeview are a few of these historic geothermal locations discussed in this guidebook. If you visit these areas, please respect private-property boundaries and observe the hot springs from the public roads. If you want to enter private land to observe or soak in a hot spring, always ask permission first. (To determine land ownership, either ask nearby homeowners or check records at the county courthouse.)

Situations constantly change. Well-known soaking spots, such as Scenic Hot Springs in Washington and Austin Hot Springs in Oregon, have recently closed to the public. Meanwhile, hot spring resorts long closed to the public, such as the one near North Bonneville on the Washington border, are being refurbished and reopened for public use.

This guidebook is divided into eight geographical sections. The Washington regions include the Olympic Peninsula, the San Juan Islands, the Washington Cascade Mountain Range, and Central Washington. The Oregon hot springs are grouped into the Oregon Cascade Mountain Range, Central Oregon, Northeast Oregon, and Southeast Oregon.

Each geographical section of the book presents detailed information on the hot springs in that area, with the chapters arranged to facilitate travel from one hot spring to the next for persons who want to plan tours to several hot springs in a single trip.

Directions and Maps

The majority of hot springs in Washington and Oregon are near paved roads or highways and require little navigational skill to locate. Each chapter of this book contains detailed directions on finding the hot springs, accompanied by a clear map. Although most of the springs should be easy to find with the map and directions in this book, you may want to obtain a topographical map before visiting some of the more isolated springs (topo maps can be obtained directly from the U.S. Geological Survey, from map-supply stores, or at many outdoor recreational stores). The name of the Forest Service or Bureau of Land Management (BLM) map most useful in finding more remote springs is included in the chapter descriptions. The following route abbreviations are used in the text: I (Interstate highway); WA or OR (Washington or Oregon State Highways); US (U.S. Highways); FR or CR (Forest or County Road).

Have a Safe Hot Spring Adventure

Although visiting the commercial hot springs resorts in Oregon and Washington requires no more preparation than you would take before traveling to any developed vacation spot, bathing in the more rustic or primitive pools requires a few precautions. Soaking in a natural hot spring is one of life's true pleasures, but be sure to plan for a safe experience.

Here's a quick checklist of things to remember before you head out on your next hot spring adventure:

• **Always test the water temperature before you get into a thermal pool.** Most people find soaks between 95° F. and 110° F. to be the most comfortable. At developed resorts in Washington and Oregon, you can usually assume that the water in the hot tubs and swimming pools is within this comfort zone. Some of the natural hot springs in Oregon and Washington, however, approach 200° F., so never take it for granted that a thermal pool will be a comfortable soak. Even hot springs in the same area may differ drastically in temperature. Some hot spring pools in the Alvord Desert of Southeastern Oregon are cool enough for a pleasant soak, whereas other thermal pools mere yards from the cooler pools could easily poach an unwary bather.

Also remember that hot springs that you've visited before can have a significantly hotter or cooler temperature on your next visit. Some hot springs are much cooler early in spring and summer, when melting snows mix with thermal water. Play it safe before you soak: Always test the water with your fingertip; then cautiously ease into the pool. The bottom of some thermal pools is much hotter than the surface, so be cautious even after you've settled in for your soak.

• **Keep your head above water in natural hot-water pools.** Some of the more popular soaking pools in Washington and Oregon have very sluggish flows, such as Baker, Kennedy, and Olympic Hot Springs. When these pools are heavily used, the water flow may be insufficient to keep the bacterial count below water-quality standards. Drinking or inhaling this water can expose you to a variety of nasty bacteria. Try to avoid inhaling water droplets or spray, especially in primitive thermal pools.

• **Don't soak by yourself.** Soaking with friends is not only more enjoyable, it's also safer.

• **Drink plenty of (nonalcoholic) fluids.** Hot-water soaks can increase your body temperature and can put abnormal stress on your heart. Drink plenty of water during your hot spring bath, and avoid alcoholic beverages, especially if you've been soaking for a long time. Lengthy thermal soaks and a high alcohol level in your bloodstream make a dangerous combination—stick to nonalcoholic beverages and save the wine or beer until you get home from your soak.

- **Don't soak in a hot pool for long periods of time if you're pregnant.**

- **Remove your jewelry before you get into thermal pools.** The sulphur found in some hot springs may quickly tarnish your favorite ring or bracelet.

- **Watch your children.** If you're soaking with your kids, make sure they are close by at all times, especially when soaking in thermal areas that have very hot pools or fragile crusts that a child could fall through.

- **Watch out for poison ivy.** The trails to several hot springs in Oregon and Washington are infamous for poison ivy infestations, especially those hot springs in the western parts of the states that are below 1,000 feet in elevation. Carson Hot Springs Resort in the Columbia River Gorge even offers a regimen of thermal soaks to help relieve inflammation if you're afflicted with poison ivy. If you happen to touch these shiny three-leafed plants, wash your skin surface immediately. It's best to wear long-sleeved shirts and pants when walking in areas that might be infested.

- **Lock your valuables in your car trunk or, better yet, leave them at home.** Unfortunately several of the more remote hot springs in Oregon and Washington have developed a reputation for vandalism. The Forest Service even has a name for the act of bashing in an automobile window and stealing your valuables—"car clouting." The parking areas at Bagby Hot Springs, Olympic Hot Springs, and Baker Hot Springs are nefarious for this kind of vandalism. If you must take valuables with you on your trip, either lock them out of sight in your trunk or take them with you in a daypack to the hot springs and then keep a close eye on them while you're soaking.

Checklist for a Great Hot Spring Visit

Preparing to visit the more luxurious hot spring resorts in Oregon and Washington requires packing little more than a swimsuit and some good books to read in the lounge chairs. But if you're planning on soaking in one of the more rustic or primitive thermal pools in the region, the following items may come in handy:

- **U.S. Forest Service or BLM Maps.** A map is essential for finding rustic hot springs.
- **Swimsuit.** Although swimsuits are optional at some rustic hot springs, take one along just in case.
- **Towel.**
- **Daypack or plastic garbage sacks.** Use to keep your clothes dry while you're soaking. Also you can use the garbage sack to pack out any trash you find when you leave a backcountry hot spring.
- **Rubber thongs or old sneakers.** Wear these to protect your feet from sharp rocks in pools.
- **Plenty of drinking water.** It's easy to get dehydrated if you soak for a long time.
- **Snack food.**
- **Sunglasses.**

- **A full tank of gas.** Be sure to fill-up, especially when visiting the remote hot springs in Eastern Oregon.
- **A hat that provides good shade protection.**
- **Sunscreen.** Use sunscreen on your nose, ears, and other areas not submerged.
- **Skin moisturizer.** Use after soaking.
- **Flashlight.** A flashlight is especially important if you're visiting some of the hot springs deep in the old-growth forests of the Oregon and Washington Cascades. Darkness falls quickly in these areas, and it's difficult and dangerous to try to find your way back to your car through the pitch-black forest.
- **Business cards or pen and paper.** You'll run into some wonderful people when you tour hot springs, and it's nice to share names and addresses with folks you meet.
- **Northwest Forest Pass.** Several of the hot springs in Oregon and Washington now require that you have a U.S. Forest Service trail pass displayed in your car at the trailhead or carried with you. The hot spring information in each chapter of this book will tell you what kind of pass you'll need and where to purchase it.

Responsible Behavior

The vast majority of people who visit Oregon and Washington hot springs know that these thermal areas are rare natural wonders, and they treat both the hot springs and other visitors with courtesy and respect. Unfortunately a few individuals haven't been as respectful of some of the more primitive pools, and their inconsiderate actions have forced restrictions to be placed on some popular hot spring areas. For example, Deer Creek Hot Springs, Terwilliger Hot Springs, McCredie Hot Springs, and several other public hot springs used to be open at nighttime. After years of alcohol-related incidents, Forest Service officials have had to close these springs to all after-dark bathing.

At some hot springs you can soak in your birthday suit.

You can do your part to protect both the fragile nature of hot spring areas as well as enhance the quality of the soaking experience for both yourself and other visitors by keeping in mind a few rules of etiquette during your visit:

- **Don't bring glass containers.** Nothing ruins a hot spring soak faster than cutting your feet on a shard of broken glass.
- **Pack out all your trash.** And pack out as much trash as you can that's been left by others.
- **Respect private-property rights.** Don't enter a hot spring on private land without being sure the owner allows public access.
- **Keep noise to a minimum.** Soaking in hot springs is an almost mystical experience to some bathers. Loud parties or blaring radios ruin the mood for everyone.
- **Watch where you walk.** Some of the hot springs in Oregon and Washington have deposited beautiful ledges of fragile minerals, which may have taken decades to build up. Walking on these delicate areas can destroy these deposits. It's also possible to break through this fragile crust, which hides scalding water just below the surface. Be especially careful when walking near the beautiful hot springs in the Alvord Desert of southeastern Oregon.
- **Follow local conventions on nudity.** Several hot springs in this book are clothing-optional, but use your own judgment before you strip. If you come to a primitive hot pool that's already occupied by clothed bathers, then either ask if it's okay to soak nude or follow the majority lead and wear your swimsuit.

What's Missing, What's Special

Hot Springs Not Included in This Guidebook

There are more than one hundred hot springs and hot-water wells in Oregon and Washington. Unfortunately many of these thermal sources are on private land that is closed to the public, are too hot for comfortable soaks, or don't produce enough water to make a decent soaking pool.

This guidebook focuses on the most accessible hot springs in Oregon and Washington, those that don't involve serious hiking. It includes both commercial resorts and secluded natural hot springs, but all these thermal areas are close to roads or are, at most, an easy walk from your vehicle.

Below are a few notes about some popular hot spring destinations that for various reasons have been omitted from this guidebook:

Kennedy Hot Springs. This warm-water soak in Washington's Glacier Peak Wilderness is a very popular hot spring destination, but the 11-mile round-trip hike precludes it from being considered an easily accessible thermal area. Besides the long hike the hot spring itself isn't as attractive as many others in the Washington Cascades. The water temperature at Kennedy is only around 92° F., much cooler than other soaks in the Washington Cascades. If you're looking for a more strenuous weekend adventure, then you might consider this trip. See the Appendix for contact information.

Scenic Hot Springs. This very popular soaking spot near Stevens Pass in the Washington Cascades was closed to the public in October of 2001. Because the private landowner had become increasingly concerned about his personal liability for allowing visitors to use this remote hot spring, he decided to prohibit further public use of the area. Volunteers had built four soaking tubs on the mountainside that captured the hot springs, and the view of the valley far below these soaking pools was truly inspiring. Unfortunately all the soaking tubs have now been dismantled, and any future use of this hot spring by the public is doubtful.

Goldmyer Hot Springs. If there were ever a competition to choose the most publicity-shy hot spring in the Oregon and Washington Cascades, then Goldmyer Hot Springs would win the blue ribbon. Goldmyer consistently requests that they not be listed in any guidebooks (although they do maintain their own detailed Web site at www.goldmyer.com). The privately owned hot spring is located a few miles north of Washington's Snoqualmie Pass. Goldmyer is a wonderful little thermal soak, but it's too difficult to reach to be considered an easily accessible hot spring. The hot water emerges from the mouth of an old coal mine, where dams have been built to create deep soaking pools. Goldmyer Hot Springs takes a maximum of twenty guests a day, and advance reservations are necessary. The drive to the trailhead to Goldmyer is long and difficult, even in high-clearance vehicles. Contact their office in Seattle (see the Appendix for phone number and address) for reservations and detailed directions to the hot springs.

North Bonneville Hot Springs Resort. Located on the Washington side of the Columbia River Gorge, this new luxury hot spring resort and spa near the town of North Bonneville is scheduled to open in June 2002. Call the main resort number (509–427–7767) for an update on this new resort.

Wind River Hot Springs. This soak on the Washington side of the Columbia River Gorge is a favorite with many veteran hot spring aficionados. A series of nice soaking pools lie on the opposite bank of the Wind River from Carson Hot Springs Resort. Unfortunately the hiking trail to these hot springs has deteriorated dramatically over the past few years. What was once a dirt trail on a cliff above the river has now become a scramble on moss-slickened rocks and ledges near the edge of the river. The local Search and Rescue department has been called several times over the past few years to rescue hikers who have twisted an ankle or broken a leg trying to reach these hot springs. The area is also infested with poison ivy. If you have the dexterity of a mountain goat, you may decide to give this hike a try, but it's definitely not for young children or anyone who is uncomfortable with boulder hopping next to a fast-flowing river. Don't attempt this hike during rainy weather, when the Wind River water level is high (usually in spring), or if it's getting dark. Better yet, forget about trying to hike to these hot springs and head a couple of hours south to Oregon's Bagby Hot Springs in the Mount Hood National Forest.

Austin Hot Springs. This vandalized eyesore was once a popular campground and soaking spot. Located about an hour's drive southeast of Portland on the North Fork of the Clackamas River, Austin Hot Springs offered a steamy soak, in which the 186° F. hot springs mixed with the cold river water. The natural soaking pools on the river banks are undeveloped, but years of illegal use of the old campground and parking area and the indiscriminate logging of the property have destroyed much of the area's beauty. Austin Hot Springs is a sad example of what happens when a popular soaking spot goes to hell. Garbage litters the old picnic and campground area near the riverbank, and sections of moldy carpet float in the once-appealing soaking pools. The current landowner has done little to deal with the mess, other than to post warnings about trespassing.

Austin Hot Springs is located about 3 miles east of River Ford Campground on Forest Road 46. If you're on your way to soak at Bagby Hot Springs, you might take a five-minute detour to check out Austin Hot Springs—from the public road you'll be able to see the steaming water on the far side of the river. Respect private property rights and don't trespass to soak here. Perhaps some day new owners will clean up the area and again allow the public to enjoy this wonderful natural thermal soak.

Hot springs along the Owyhee River. Several nice thermal soaks and warm waterfalls are located along the banks of the Owyhee River in extreme southeastern Oregon. Reaching most of these soaks, including the popular Three Forks Hot Springs and Echo Rock Hot Springs, requires a long day hike or fording or rafting down the Owyhee River.

Author's Favorite Hot Springs

Most Remote: Willow Creek Hot Springs

It may be a contradiction to feature a "most remote" hot spring in a guidebook that emphasizes easily accessible thermal soaks, but Willow Creek Hot Springs in southeastern Oregon is both accessible and remote. Reaching this soak in the high desert of southeast Oregon requires a long day's drive from almost anywhere in the state, and the final few miles of dirt road can be impassable in wet weather. Those visitors who endure the bumpy journey will be rewarded with twin soaking pools surrounded by an endless sagebrush prairie.

Scenic soaking pools at Willow Creek Hot Springs.

Most Historic: Hot Lake

A majority of hot springs in Washington and Oregon have interesting histories, but Hot Lake in northeastern Oregon certainly has the oldest pedigree. First visited by European explorers with the Astor Expedition in 1812, Hot Lake later became a popular stop for weary travelers on the Oregon trail in the 1840s. Some historians consider the hotel built at Hot Lake in 1864 to have been the first commercial building in the United States to use geothermal energy for space heating. Even after its demise the old resort continues to attract the curious. The massive brick sanitarium, which now sits abandoned near the hot springs, generates some of Oregon's best ghost stories.

Best for Families: Kah-Nee-Ta Resort

Located on the Warm Springs Indian Reservation on the sunny east slope of the Oregon Cascades, Kah-Nee-Ta Resort has more family-oriented activities than many resorts located much closer to urban areas. For children there's the 140-foot-long water slide and the Olympic-sized swimming pool, along with the chance to sleep in a genuine Native American teepee. Horseback riding, kayaking, volleyball, hiking, and bike riding attract teenagers, whereas the 18-hole golf course, fish-filled river, gourmet restaurant, and a casino will satisfy mom and dad's desire for more adult recreation.

Best Nude Soak: Doe Bay Resort

Several hot springs in Oregon and Washington are clothing-optional, but Doe Bay Resort on Orcas Island gets my nod for the best bath in your birthday suit. The mellow atmosphere and well-maintained soaking facilities lend a sense of security to nude bathers that is sometimes lacking at other hot springs. Doe Bay features three soaking tubs, a sauna big

Kah-Nee-Ta's swimming pool, advertised as "Central Oregon's Largest Pool."

enough to hold two dozen of your swimsuit-free friends, and a secluded nude beach where a curious sea otter in Puget Sound would be the only neighbor likely to catch a glimpse of your bare buns.

Most Romantic: Lithia Springs Inn

Combine private, two-person whirlpools in the cozy cottages at Lithia Springs Inn with nearby gourmet restaurants, add the world-famous Oregon Shakespeare Festival, and you have a perfect recipe for romance. Honeymooners and retired couples alike credit the inn's silky-soft mineral water for turbocharging their relationships. One couple wrote in the inn's guest book that their "carnal knowledge" had been reawakened by the thermal springs. The many cultural attractions in nearby Ashland add perfect venues for building a weekend of memories with your significant other.

Most Eclectic: Soap Lake

The dry prairies of central Washington seem a strange place to find a once-booming spa town, but Soap Lake is filled with such eccentricities. The mineral-rich waters of the town's namesake have been praised for their abilities to cure everything from snakebite to baldness (not to mention the legend of the water resurrecting a dead cowboy). A sizable contingent of immigrants from Eastern Europe take up residence near the lake during summer, both to soak in and to drink the celebrated water. The citizens of Soap Lake are constantly dreaming up ways to boost their small town, promoting everything from a mid-summer health fair and canoe race to community mud baths on the lakeshore.

Washington Hot Springs

Sol Duc Hot Springs Resort

Contact information:
Sol Duc Hot Springs Resort
P.O. Box 2169
Port Angeles, WA 98362-0283
(360) 327–3583
www.northolympic.com/solduc/

General description: A commercial resort nestled in a valley of the Northern Hemisphere's only temperate rain forest.

Location: Olympic Peninsula, 40 miles west of Port Angeles on the banks of the Sol Duc River in Olympic National Park.

Development: Sol Duc Hot Springs has been developed commercially for close to one hundred years. Current facilities include a restaurant, cabins, hot soaking pools, and a cold-water swimming pool.

Best times to visit: The resort is open from late April through October. Because Sol Duc is in a temperate rain forest, expect cloudy and wet weather anytime. July and August are usually the driest (and busiest) months. Midweek is less crowded, as is the period before Memorial Day and after Labor Day. Cabins are often booked weeks in advance, so make your reservations as early as possible.

Restrictions: Swimsuits are required in the swimming and soaking pools. Cabin fees include use of the pools; other guests must pay a day-use fee. There's a required two-night minimum stay during holidays. The cabins and lodge are non-smoking.

Access: Any vehicle can travel the paved highway and blacktop county road to the hot springs.

Water temperature: The three soaking pools are kept between 101° and 106° F. The cold-water swimming pool averages 78° F.

Sol Duc Hot Springs

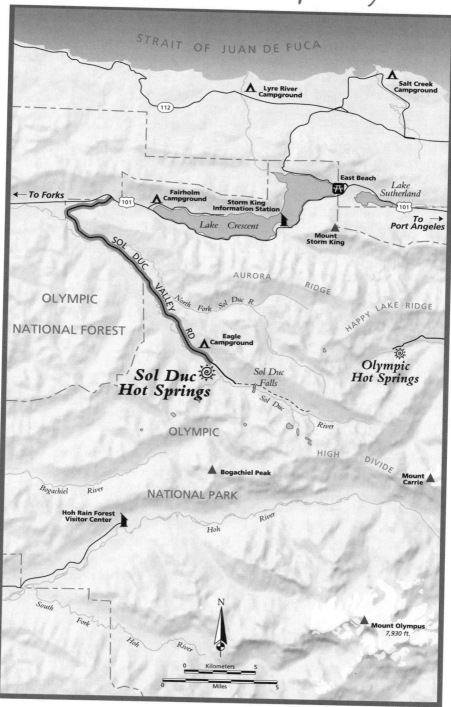

STRAIT OF JUAN DE FUCA

Lyre River
Campground

Salt Creek
Campground

112

East Beach

Lake
Sutherland

← To Forks

101

Fairholm
Campground

Storm King
Information Station

Lake   Crescent

Mount
Storm King

To →
Port Angeles

101

SOL DUC VALLEY RD

AURORA   RIDGE

North Fork Sol Duc R.

HAPPY LAKE RIDGE

OLYMPIC

NATIONAL FOREST

Eagle
Campground

**Sol Duc
Hot Springs**

Sol Duc
Falls

Sol Duc

River

*Olympic
Hot Springs*

OLYMPIC

HIGH   DIVIDE

Bogachiel Peak

Mount
Carrie

Bogachiel   River

NATIONAL PARK

Hoh Rain Forest
Visitor Center

River

Hoh

Mount Olympus
7,930 ft.

South

Fork

Hoh   River

N

Kilometers   5

Miles   5

Services: The resort has a snack bar, a gift shop, and a small grocery store in the main lodge. The Springs Restaurant provides breakfast and dinner, and poolside lunches are served. Massage therapy is available.

Accommodations: Sol Duc has thirty-three cabins available, six with kitchens. The cabins with kitchen facilities are less scenic. Many guests choose to stay in the more remote cabins, without kitchen facilities, and eat their meals in the lodge restaurant (oatmeal with fresh berries for breakfast and steelhead trout for dinner are favorite choices). The resort also has twenty RV spots across the Sol Duc River from the cabins. Tent camping is available less than a mile away at the Sol Duc Campground, maintained by the National Park Service. The campground has more than eighty tent and RV sites (no hookups). The campground is available on a first-come first-served basis, so arrive early in the day to grab a spot for your tent or RV. During summer park rangers often give an evening lecture at the campground on the natural history of the surrounding area.

Map: Washington State Highway Map.

Finding the springs: From Port Angeles drive 27 miles west on US 101. (The final 10 miles of this drive skirts the shores of Lake Crescent.) Turn left onto the Sol Duc Valley Road (you'll see a large sign for Sol Duc Hot Springs at the junction with US 101). Drive 12 miles on this two-lane blacktop road through beautiful groves of fir and cedar to the Sol Duc Hot Springs Resort.

Overview: All of Sol Duc Resort's soaking opportunities are clustered behind the main lodge. (Diners in the Springs Restaurant have a front-row view of the bathers.) Two circular hot pools, both about 20 feet in diameter, are the focus for most visitors. The pools, which are about 2 feet deep, are filled with natural hot water that measures 101° to 105° F. A hot-water fountain gurgles from a platform in the center of the pool closest to the lodge. A smaller wading pool about 6 inches deep lies adjacent to the soaking pool. The hot pools are drained and cleaned every night after closing.

Farthest from the lodge is the cold-water swimming pool, which is 100 feet long by 30 feet wide and 2 to 10 feet deep. This chlorinated pool usually measures a brisk 74° to 78° F. The chilly swimming-pool water is especially popular with children, while adults can keep an eye on their clans from the comfort of the warm soaking pools.

A covered overhang near the dressing room and showers provides a dry place for towels. You'll probably need to use that dry area as Sol Duc typically receives 150 inches of rain a year—that's more than *10 feet* of annual rainfall. Some visitors to Sol Duc have been known to open an umbrella above them while soaking

Sol Duc Hot Springs, deep in the Olympic Peninsula rain forest.

in the hot pools, keeping the cold drizzle off their heads and shoulders while they contently steam beneath.

History: Theodore Moritz was the first European to discover Sol Duc Hot Springs. During a hunting trip in the 1880s, Moritz came upon a Native American in the woods who had broken his leg. Moritz nursed the man back to health, who returned the favor by telling Moritz of hot springs deep in the woods that were used by members of his tribe to treat their illnesses. Moritz followed the directions to the hot springs, where he saw many tribesmen bathing in the hot water. Moritz filed a claim on the land and built a crude trail from the hot springs to Lake Crescent, then settled in on his new property, building a cabin near the springs and carving a soaking tub from a cedar log. Word of the hot springs spread to other settlers, and Moritz hosted a steadily increasing number of visitors who came to soak in the healing waters.

One of the visitors to Moritz's homestead was Michael Earles, a wealthy lumber baron from Seattle. In 1903 Earles was diagnosed with a life-threatening disease, and physicians had little hope for his survival. One doctor suggested that Earles travel to the famous Carlsbad hot springs in Czechoslovakia for treatment. Earles's health was failing rapidly, and he felt that he was too weak to make the European journey. He had heard of the rustic hot springs resort on the Olympic Peninsula and decided to see if the springs would be helpful for his malady. After a few weeks of soaking in the hot springs at Sol Duc, Earles emerged "as good as new," according to one newspaper article. Earles was so impressed with the curative power of the hot springs that upon the death of Theodore Moritz in 1910, he purchased the property.

Earles transformed the little homestead into what may have been the most lavish resort in the Pacific Northwest. The main attraction to Earles's new resort was the Sol Duc Hot Springs Hotel, which opened in 1912. The four-story hotel was 160 feet long, 80 feet wide, and surrounded on three sides by a veranda 20 feet deep and 400 feet long. The building featured 165 bedrooms, a laundry room, an ice plant, and its own power plant. A massive stone-and-brick fireplace, an electric organ, and a dining room that seated 150 greeted guests entering the main lobby. Living fir trees served as the main supports for the hotel. A ballroom provided a forum for orchestras that Earles occasionally invited to the resort. Guests at the hotel relaxed while "music for turkey trots, tangos, or waltzes floated out to the long veranda on summer evenings as merrymakers splashed in the nearby pools while the sedate sat in chairs, gazing at the background of stars, mountains, and river."

Connected to the hotel by a covered walk was a three-story sanatorium, staffed with a resident physician, several nurses, and massage therapists and attendants. The sanatorium attracted the sick and infirm, who would spend weeks under the care of the physician. Next to the sanatorium was a bathhouse for recreational soaking and swimming. A gymnasium and several cottages were also scattered on the well-manicured grounds. Golf links, tennis courts, croquet fields, a movie theater, bowling alleys, and billiard rooms were available for the pleasure of hotel guests. Each resort guest was given his or her own cup to drink the mineral water from a bubbling hot springs fountain.

Earles promoted the resort to the Seattle community as "The Carlsbad of America." In a 1912 brochure announcing the opening of the new hotel, Earles lauded the miraculous healing qualities of the thermal water:

> The rheumatic diathesis, in common with hepatic, gastric, renal and every form of blood and skin diseases, each and all, succumbed with remarkable rapidity to the benignant energies of the water . . . it would not be transcending the truth to state that all diseases are cured or largely benefited by the wonderful energy of these waters . . . health waits for those who may come and partake of this—life's elixir.

The elegance of the Sol Duc Hot Springs Hotel was short-lived. Four years to the month after its opening, the hotel burned to the ground when sparks from a defective flue caught the wooden shingles on fire. A strong west wind blew the flames to most of the other buildings on the property, destroying the sanatorium, bathhouse, and cottages. One guest at the hotel reported that the fire short-circuited the electric organ, which then played Beethoven's "Funeral March"

The majestic Sol Duc Hot Springs Hotel in 1912. PHOTO: BURT KELLOGG COLLECTION

until the fire finally burned through its electrical wires. Within three short hours the raging fire had destroyed the resort.

The tragic fire of 1916 ended Sol Duc's fame as one of the most elegant destination resorts for wealthy patrons from Seattle. Michael Earles died three years after the fire, and the property was sold soon thereafter. Over the next fifty years, the resort had several owners who rebuilt the pool and some of the cottages, but the grandeur of the hotel and sanatorium of 1912 was never again realized.

In 1966 the owner of the resort sold the 320 acres, which included the hot springs, to the National Park Service for $880,000. For the past thirty-five years, Sol Duc Hot Springs has been operated by private concessionaires on long-term leases from Olympic National Park.

Area attractions: Sol Duc Hot Springs is a great location for accessing some of Olympic National Park's nicest views and hiking trails. Sol Duc Falls is about a mile past the resort and campground. Stop at the overlook to see this 60-foot waterfall dropping into a narrow canyon. One short (but strenuous) hiking trail starts at the resort and climbs about two and a half miles to trout-filled Mink Lake. Another memorable hike that anyone can take is the Ancient Groves Nature Trail, an easy half-mile loop through a giant Douglas fir forest. The trail starts about 3 miles north of Sol Duc Hot Springs on the road leading back to US 101. For more insight into the ecology of the rain forest, head back to US 101 and drive west to the Hoh Rain Forest Visitor Center.

2

Olympic Hot Springs

Contact information:
Olympic National Park
Wilderness Information Center
3002 Mt. Angeles Road
Port Angeles, WA 98362
(360) 452–0300
Hot Springs trail conditions: www.nps.gov/olym/wic/trailrpt.htm#OLYMPIC

General description: A half-dozen wilderness soaking pools sprinkled along a hillside above Boulder Creek in Olympic National Park.

Location: Olympic Peninsula, 21 miles southwest of Port Angeles in Olympic National Park.

Development: Olympic Hot Springs was at one time a popular commercial resort, but all remnants of these developments were removed by the National Park Service in the 1970s. Volunteer-built rock-and-log dams enclose the current natural soaking pools.

Best times to visit: Weekends and holidays are usually very busy—it's not uncommon to see thirty or forty cars in the trailhead parking area. Winter may be the best time to visit, when the crowds are few and the steaming water provides a dramatic contrast to surrounding snowbanks. The soaking pools are often a bit cool in springtime, when cold water from snowmelt mixes with the thermal water.

Restrictions: Because the hot springs are located within Olympic National Park, you'll need to purchase a National Park Pass. (Purchase this at the guard station near the mouth of the Elwha Valley.) Camping permits are also required if you plan to stay overnight at the camping area near the hot springs. Camping is allowed only in the designated campsite.

Olympic Hot Springs

The National Park Service doesn't condone nudity in the soaking pools, but it isn't banned. Actually the Park Service doesn't condone soaking of any kind in the hot springs, because the sluggish water can contain high levels of coliform bacteria. Visitors routinely ignore both warnings, and Park Service personnel tolerate both bathing and nudity. There's usually a mix of clothed and nude bathers in the soaking pools.

Access: Any vehicle can make the trip to the trailhead for Olympic Hot Springs, except for a few weeks in winter when snow blocks the last 4 miles to the trailhead. Cross-country skiers are the main winter visitors when snow blocks the lower road. Bicycles are allowed on the 2.4-mile section of trail to the Boulder Creek Bridge, so consider bringing your mountain bike along.

Water temperature: The temperature in the soaking pools varies from 85° F. to 105° F.

Services: No services are available at the hot springs. Groceries, gas, and lodging are available in Port Angeles, 21 miles northeast.

Accommodations: Boulder Creek Campground is 0.25 mile north of the hot springs. (A camping permit is required to stay here.) More civilized accommodations are available in Port Angeles. Sol Duc Hot Springs resort has cabins available for rent in the summer months. It's situated about 30 miles west of Olympic Hot Springs off US 101.

Maps: Olympic National Park map, Olympic Hot Springs & Camping Area leaflet (both available at Elwha Ranger Station).

Finding the springs: From Port Angeles drive west on US 101 for 10 miles to the Elwha River Road (also called the Olympic Hot Springs Road). Turn left and drive to the entrance gate for Olympic National Park. The gate isn't always staffed, but if it is, pay a National Park entrance fee and pick up a brochure about the trail to Olympic Hot Springs. From the entrance gate drive 8 miles on a winding road that ends at the parking area for the Appleton Pass Trailhead (the last 4 miles of this road switchbacks up a steep hill from Mills Lake). From the trailhead it's a 2.2-mile hike on an abandoned blacktop road to the Boulder Creek campground. Cross the footbridge over Boulder Creek (stop and look upstream for a great view of a waterfall), turn left, and head on the trail that parallels Boulder Creek downstream. In less than five minutes, you'll start seeing the soaking pools on the side of the trail.

Overview: Locals used to call the area "Triple 21 Hot Springs"—2,100 feet in elevation, 21 miles from Port Angeles, and 21 hot springs seeping out of the hillside above Boulder Creek. Those twenty-one hot springs seeps still exist, but only

An enticing soaking pool at Olympic Hot Springs.

seven of them are collected into soaking pools. You'll encounter these seven pools every 50 to 100 yards after crossing the footbridge and taking the path to the left. Sometimes the hot pool will be obvious (only a few yards off the trail), but a couple of them are hidden higher up the ridge. Look for footpaths heading up the hill and little hot-water creeks to give you hints as to where these hidden pools might be.

The first soaking pool appears just above the hiking trail about 100 yards from the footbridge. Rocks and logs enclose the spring, which is about 6 feet wide by 15 feet long and 1.5 to 2 feet deep. Hot springs bubble up in this pool, as well as trickle in from a rock fissure. A river birch shades most of the pool, which has a rock and silt bottom.

Don't be too hasty to jump in the first pool you see—the best soaking pools are the farthest down the trail. Past the first pool on the left down close to the creek is a small soaking pool (the "meadow pool"). This pool is often overlooked because it's the only one not on the uphill side of the trail.

Uphill from the trail past the meadow pool are three other small soaking pools, each about 30 yards above (and hidden from) the trail. The sixth pool is actually a double family-size soaker right by the trail. These twin pools are about 20 feet across. The last pool (and to many folks the best) is past the family pools. Walk about 50 yards and then turn on the steep footpath headed up the ridge. The trail climbs about 300 feet to a soaking pool in the middle of a hot-water creek dammed with logs and rocks. This 6-foot by 15-foot pool holds a half dozen or more bathers and tends to be the hottest (and most popular) soaking pool in the series.

The hot spring water entering the seven pools tends to stay at a fairly constant temperature, but cold water from snowmelt and heavy rainstorms can dilute the pools. In rare cases during spring, this cold-water runoff can cool the pools to the point that they are uncomfortable for soaking, but most of the year this isn't a concern.

Rangers for Olympic National Park regularly patrol the area, picking up trash and seeing that partying is kept under control. It can be a bit disconcerting the first time you see Park Service personnel in their uniforms and badges standing next to a pool full of naked bathers, but everyone seems to be pretty mellow about the situation.

History: Native Americans in the area have long had a legend about the creation of both Olympic Hot Springs and nearby Sol Duc Hot Springs:

> Two "dragon-like creatures" with a mutual hatred for one another engaged in a mighty and desperate battle. There was no victor as both were evenly matched. Admitting defeat, each of the creatures crawled into their separate caves where they still weep hot tears of mortification.

The hot tears of these dragons are said to be the hot water bubbling to the surface in these two hot springs.

The first European to discover Olympic Hot Springs was Andrew Jacobsen, who stumbled across the steaming waters in 1892. Jacobsen was alarmed by the sight of the hot water, fearing it was a sign that the mountain was going to blow up. He beat a hasty retreat down the Elwha Valley away from the hot springs. Apparently no one else visited the site for the next fifteen years, until William Everett rediscovered the hot springs in 1907. Unlike Jacobsen, Everett had no fear of the mountain erupting and filed a homestead claim on the hot springs property.

Everett built a cabin and bathhouse near the springs and moved his family to the little homestead. In spite of the arduous 12-mile hike or horseback ride from the Port Angeles road to the hot springs, visitors soon started arriving at Everett's small bathhouse to soak in the hot water. In 1908 Everett decided to build some tent frames and rent overnight accommodations to the visitors. He also built a larger bathhouse containing six wooden tubs that he carved out of cedar logs. A lodge with dining room was built in 1917, followed by a swimming pool 75 feet long and 25 feet wide. Cabins were added to the property in 1920, the same year that Everett's daughter married Harry Schoffel. Schoffel took over management

Olympic Hot Springs pool and cabins circa 1932.   PHOTO: BURT KELLOGG COLLECTION

of the resort in 1924 and spent six years building an even larger lodge on the property, complete with a dining room, a kitchen, and ten sleeping rooms. An additional ten sleeping rooms were added in 1932.

Visits to Olympic Hot Springs increased dramatically in 1930, when the U.S. Forest Service built 12 miles of new road from the highway to the little resort. Gone were the days when visitors had to walk or ride on horseback to get to the hot springs. Schoffel built an Olympic-sized swimming pool and additional cabins near Boulder Creek behind the lodge to handle the increased visitor load. Resort business boomed for the next decade.

In January 1940 tragedy struck the resort when the lodge caught fire. The lodge was constructed almost entirely of cedar, and the fire quickly destroyed the building. Fortunately the fire didn't spread to the swimming pool or cabins, but it did mark the beginning of the end of Olympic Hot Springs' commercial success.

Shortly after the fire, the federal government acquired the property and incorporated it into Olympic National Park. The resort was leased back to Schoffel, but new Federal requirements were put in place. The Forest Service required Schoffel to use only chlorinated fresh water in the swimming pool, which drastically reduced the number of tourists who have visited the resort because of the natural hot springs water.

The Schoffel family continued to manage the resort until 1966, when the National Park Service decided not to renew their lease. The resort was closed, and the abandoned buildings collapsed under the weight of heavy winter snows. In 1972 the National Park Service decided to let the area revert to its natural state and removed all buildings from the area. At present the only signs that Olympic Hot Springs was once a bustling resort are a few cisterns and pieces of iron pipe near some of the springs that were used to gather the hot water for use in the old swimming pool.

Area attractions: Olympic National Park has a wide variety of outdoor opportunities. Stop at the main Olympic National Park Visitor Center in Port Angeles to plan your trip. One of the most popular summer drives is the 17-mile road up to Hurricane Ridge, one of the highest spots in the park, with awesome views and some nice day hikes. The Hoh Rain Forest Visitor Center is also extremely popular. Located on the west side of the park, this visitor center has wonderful displays telling the story of the only temperate rain forest in the Northern Hemisphere. Nearby are easy hikes through moss-covered cedars and firs.

Doe Bay Village Resort

Contact information:
Doe Bay Village Resort
P.O. Box 437
Olga, WA 98279
(360) 376–2291
www.doebay.com

Ferry schedules to and from Orcas Island:
Washington State Ferries
Colman Dock/Pier 52
801 Alaskan Way
Seattle, WA 98104
(206) 464–6400
www.wsdot.wa.gov/ferries/current

General description: A rustic New Age retreat with clothing-optional soaking tubs overlooking a peaceful cove in Washington's San Juan Islands.

Location: Southeast end of Orcas Island, 19 miles from the Orcas ferry dock.

Development: The forty-five-acre property was originally developed as a ferry landing in the late 1800s. Current developments include a variety of sleeping accommodations, a general store, a restaurant, a massage house, a sauna, and soaking tubs.

Best times to visit: Doe Bay Resort is open year-round, although the Doe Bay Café may be closed during winter months (call ahead to find out current status). According to a sign near the soaking area, the hot tubs and sauna are open 9ISH A.M. TO 10ISH P.M. Weekends, holidays, and summer are busiest. Call well in advance of your trip for cabin reservations or to reserve one of the better camping spots next to the water. It's best to take a ferry early in the day from Anacortes

Doe Bay Village Resort

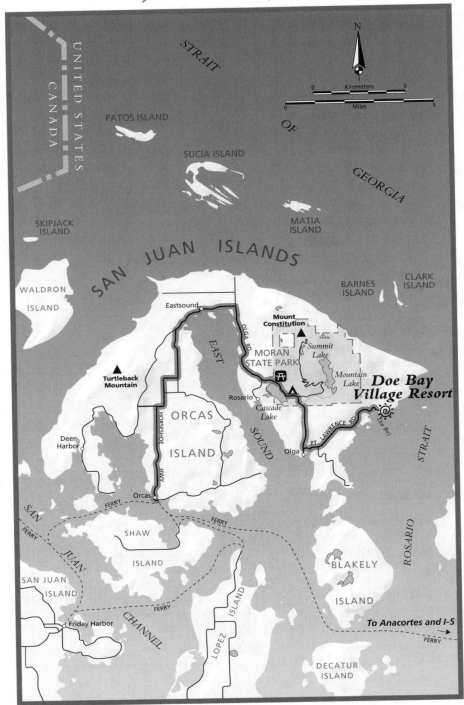

to Orcas Island to ensure you arrive at the resort during daylight hours—the heavily forested resort is not well lit, and you can have a difficult time finding your assigned cabin or camping spot in the darkness.

Restrictions: The use of the mineral-water soaking tubs and the sauna is restricted to overnight guests and to visitors who pay a day-use fee. The hot tub and sauna area is clothing-optional—most guests soak in the nude. A clothing-optional beach dubbed "little Miami" is also available. Nudity is not permitted outside the nude beach, hot tubs, or sauna area. No minors under the age of eighteen are allowed in the soaking tub area after 6:00 P.M. No pets are permitted from June 15 to September 15. No dogs, alcohol, cigarettes, or glass containers are allowed in the hot-tub area. No smoking is allowed in the cabins.

Access: Any vehicle can make the trip on the paved roads that lead from the ferry terminal across Orcas Island to Doe Bay Resort.

Water temperature: Two hot tubs contain natural mineral water that's piped from a 300-foot-deep well, then heated to 105° to 110° F. The adjacent cold-water pool is a bracing 52° F.

Services: A small selection of groceries can be found in the store just off the lobby of the Doe Bay Café. A variety of massage therapies can be scheduled with the resident professional therapist. Guided sea-kayak tours of Doe Bay are offered, and mountain-bike rentals are available.

Accommodations: If you're seeking fancy digs, head down the road about 10 miles from Doe Bay to the elegant Rosario Resort, but if you want to revitalize your spirit in a rustic natural setting, then Doe Bay Resort may just be your place. Choose from a variety of sleeping options, which include primitive campsites with views of Otter Cove, octagonal yurts with skylights and futon beds that would be the envy of Mongolian tribesmen, and simply furnished cabins (some with kitchens). Adventurous souls can request a sleeping space on a wooden platform placed high in a tree, or you can join fellow travelers in the group hostel. Camping and RV spots are also available.

Two community bathrooms and shower houses are provided for guests at campsites and in those cabins without toilets. Guests without cooking facilities can use a community kitchen. Guests often bring their own food to the resort and then write their names on their perishables before placing them in the community refrigerator with the provisions of other visitors.

Maps: The Washington State Highway Map is adequate, but you might want to pick up a more detailed map of Orcas Island in one of the free visitor guides available in the information racks on the Washington ferries.

Finding the springs: From I–5 north of Mount Vernon take exit 230 and head west on WA 20 to Anacortes. Follow the signs in Anacortes to the San Juan Island ferry. The ferry ride from Anacortes to Orcas Island usually takes about an hour, during which you'll have a wonderful view of several of the islands of the San Juans.

Once the ferry lands at Orcas Island, take the Horseshoe Highway for about 8 miles to the town of Eastsound. (Keep alert on this drive: Orcas Island is popular with bicyclists and deer, both of which can suddenly appear on the narrow winding roads.) Drive through Eastsound, proceeding east for about a mile until you come to Olga Road. Turn right on Olga Road, and drive 10 miles south to the entrance to Moran State Park. Stay on Olga Road and drive the 2 miles through the state park (you'll pass through a narrow arch at the park boundary). Continue beyond the state park on Olga Road for another 2.5 miles, and turn left at the Olga Café onto Pt. Lawrence Road. Drive 3.5 miles on Pt. Lawrence Road until you see the Doe Bay Resort sign on the right. Turn into the resort and drive about 50 yards to a parking area near the Doe Bay Café. Park your car and go into the lobby of the café to register. If you arrive late at night and the café is closed, your registration information and map will be waiting for you in a slot by the door of the café—go to your cabin or campsite and settle up your account the next morning.

Overview: The brochure given to guests contains a line that sums up the culture of this laid-back retreat: "Contrary to popular belief, Doe Bay Resort does not require guests to don tie-dye garb." Visitors describe Doe Bay as a "neo-hippie" island retreat, with its roots extending back to the 1960s and 1970s, when a "human potential center" named the Polarity Institute was based on the property. The current managers warn that "Doe Bay is not for everyone, yet if you enjoy simplicity, nature, and relaxing, Doe Bay is the place for you." The resort owners definitely have New Age roots—they also manage a yoga ashram in Virginia.

The resort welcomes guests of all persuasions, although you'll discover a strong liberal leaning in the politics of most. You may find yourself soaking in the hot tubs next to newlyweds on their first visit to Orcas Island or next to a Doe Bay veteran who has visited the resort every summer for the past twenty years to meditate and recharge her batteries.

The three spring-fed soaking tubs are reached along a footpath that skirts Otter Cove. Located on the opposite side of the cove from the Doe Bay Café, the tubs are sheltered by trees as well as by a translucent plastic roof that often drips with condensation from morning fogs. The three side-by-side soaking pools are each about 6 feet square and 3 feet deep. Two of the tubs are filled with mineral water heated to 105° to 110° F., whereas the third, a cold-water pool, provides a respite from the thermal soaks. A spacious three-level sauna that can easily hold a

The Doe Bay Café.

dozen bodies is just a few steps from the pool. The pool and sauna area is often lively with conversation and laughter, especially in the evenings, but the atmosphere never gets as rowdy as at it does at some public hot springs.

In between soaks you can enjoy excellent vegetarian and seafood meals at the Doe Bay Café. With lava lamps in the windows and Grateful Dead music playing in the background, the café reflects the true counterculture spirit of the resort. Breakfast features daily specials as well as a continental buffet; dinner usually has one or two seafood specials (beer and wine are also available). Pick a window seat with a good view of Otter Cove—during your meal the college-age waiter may point out a family of sea otters frolicking in the calm waters below your window.

History: The land around Doe Bay was at one time the site of a fishing village for the Lummi tribe of Native Americans. The first Europeans homesteaded near Doe Bay in 1871, and the first post office was opened in 1881. In 1908 a new post office and general store were built near Otter Cove. This building, which is on the National Historic Register, is now home to the Doe Bay Café. For decades the store and post office bustled with local fishermen and travelers arriving and departing from a nearby ferry dock. In 1953 the post office at Doe Bay closed. Since then the property has been the site of an artist colony, a human potential center, and a health spa. The current resort is infused with the spirit of all these past activities.

Area attractions: Horseshoe-shaped Orcas Island is the largest island in the San Juans, encompassing 54 square miles. Moran State Park, the largest state park in Washington, is situated 6 miles north of Doe Bay Resort. A popular day trip is the hike or drive to the summit of Mount Constitution, which towers 2,409 feet above sea level and features an awesome view of the San Juan Islands and Olympic and Cascade Mountains. Elegant Rosario Resort, on Cascade Bay northwest of Moran State Park, features a 35,000-square-foot mansion built by the ex-mayor of Seattle, Robert Moran. Free concerts are often given at the mansion on a majestic 1,972-pipe organ. Eastsound, the largest community on Orcas Island, is home to a nice selection of restaurants.

Baker Hot Spring

Contact information:
Mount Baker–Snoqualmie National Forest
Baker Ranger District
810 State Route 20
Sedro-Woolley, WA 98284
(360) 856–5700
www.fs.fed.us/r6/mbs

Baker Lake Resort
46110 East Main Street
Concrete, WA 98237
(888) 711–3033

General description: An easily accessible soaking pool in a forest glen surrounded by cedars and Douglas fir.

Location: Washington Cascades, 55 miles northeast of Mount Vernon in the Mount Baker–Snoqualmie National Forest.

Development: Undeveloped, except for the rock work done by volunteers to create the soaking pool.

Best times to visit: The hot spring is fairly empty during the mornings, midweek, and wintertime. Avoid evenings and holidays unless you're looking to soak with a large (and sometimes rowdy) crowd. Weekends are popular with students from Western Washington University in nearby Bellingham, as well as with a few Canadians crossing the border to sample American hot springs.

Restrictions: The Forest Service's current policy is to "allow but not promote or encourage" the use of Baker Hot Spring. The Forest Service also claims that the slow-moving water in the soaking pool often fails to meet water-quality standards for fecal-coliform levels. Bathe at your own risk.

Baker Hot Spring

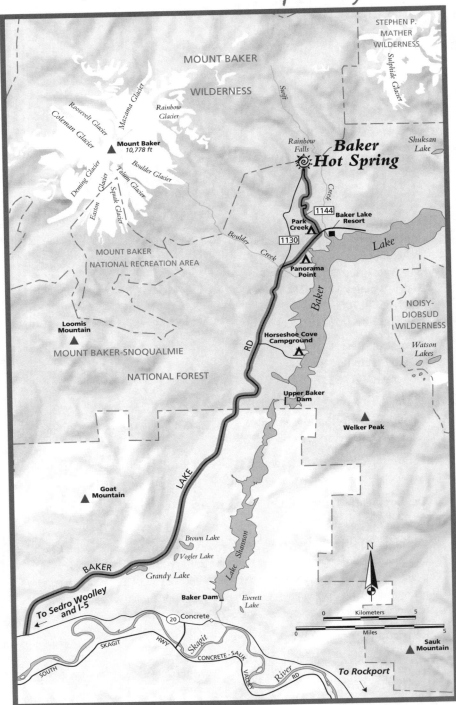

Unlike several hot springs on public land in Oregon and Washington, Baker Hot Spring has no nighttime soaking restrictions. The Forest Service has responded to a number of incidents of vandalism to cars in the parking area, broken beer bottles in the soaking pool, and obnoxious behavior by fellow bathers. It is hoped that the inconsiderate actions of a small minority of visitors won't force the Forest Service to impose additional restrictions on the use of this pleasant soaking spot.

You'll usually find a mix of nude and clothed bathers at Baker Hot Spring, so let your own judgment guide you on proper soaking attire.

Access: Most vehicles can travel the washboarded and potholed Forest Road the final few miles to the hot spring, but high-clearance vehicles are advised. FR 1144 is sometimes closed in winter when snow gets too deep, although during mild winters the road may be open year-round. In heavy snow years the last 2 or 3 miles of road may be blocked. Winter soaking enthusiasts pack their snowshoes or cross-country skis to traverse the final leg of the trip during snowy winters.

Water temperature: The pool temperature averages 100° to 105° F, although it is sometimes cooler during spring snowmelt, when cold water from an adjacent stream mixes with the hot spring.

Services: None available at the hot spring. Food and gas are available during the summer months at the Baker Lake Resort or year-round in the towns of Hamilton and Concrete on WA 20.

Accommodations: Park Creek Campground is situated near the intersection of FR 1144 and the Baker Lake Road (about 3 miles from Baker Hot Spring). Boulder Creek Campground and Panorama Point Creek Campground are also nearby. During the summer months you can rent a cabin or park your RV at the ninety-acre Baker Lake Resort. Acquired by Puget Sound Energy in 1998, the resort is on the west bank of Baker Lake, which the utility uses as a storage reservoir for summer hydropower needs.

Maps: Washington State Highway Map, Mount Baker–Snoqualmie National Forest Map, USGS Mount Shuksan Quadrangle.

Finding the spring: From I–5 north of Mount Vernon, take Exit 230 east to WA 20. Drive 23 miles east on WA 20; then turn right at Milepost 82 onto Baker Lake Road. Drive 20.5 miles up Baker Lake Road to the intersection of Baker Lake Resort (on the right) and FR 1144 (on the left). If you need any supplies, stop at the grocery store at Baker Lake Resort (don't forget to pick up some drinking water). Turn left onto FR 1144, and drive for 3.1 miles to a wide turnout overlooking a valley. (This section of road is often very bumpy from all the potholes—take your time.) Park your car in the turnout, and look for a footpath on the inside bend of the road headed up a small hill. The hot spring is located about 300 yards from the parking area. (It's a gentle walk once you get up the first 50 feet.)

You can also take another route to the hot spring, which is usually a better (but longer) road than the bumpy 3.1 miles from Baker Lake Resort on FR 1144. When you leave WA 20, drive 18 miles up Baker Lake Road. Turn left onto FR 1130 (Marten Lake Road) just past the Boulder Creek Bridge. Drive 1.5 miles to a junction, and keep right. Drive 2.5 miles from the junction to FR 1144. Proceed 0.5 miles on FR 1144 to the turnout and overlook. Look for the unmarked hiking trail to Baker Hot Spring on the right.

Overview: After being jostled on the bumpy forest road that leads to the parking area, you'll savor the hushed quiet of the footpath that passes through a grove of old-growth cedar trees. The ten-minute walk ends in a cathedral of Douglas fir, maple, and cedar that surrounds the 15-foot-diameter soaking pool.

Baker Hot Spring can easily hold a dozen or more bathers, and unless it's really crowded you can stretch out and even paddle around a bit in the 2-foot-deep water. The hot spring water bubbles up in several places in the gravel bottom of the soaking pool. The pool temperature is about 104° F. at its hottest, but cools down slightly away from bubbling inlets. There's a strong odor of sulphur in the water, and the sulphur smell will linger on your skin and hair long after you

Baker Hot Spring, an easy ten-minute walk from the parking area.

return to your car.

If left undisturbed, the water in the pool is crystal clear, but usually bathers stir up the sediments on the pool bottom. The water then takes on a unique bluish-gray milky color.

Candle wax on the rocks and logs surrounding the soaking pool testifies to nighttime gatherings, some of which can get pretty wild. You'll often find some trash and a discarded towel or two along the trail or near the pool. Take a garbage sack with you and pack out any trash to help keep this well-visited hot spring worth visiting.

History: In the 1890s a prospector named Joe Morovitz built a soaking pool around the natural hot springs. The springs were known as Morovitz Hot Springs for many years. No further development occurred until the 1960s or 1970s, when the Skagit Alpine Club built a four-person soaking tub, changing room, and outhouse near the springs. In 1978 the Forest Service removed all manmade structures because of concerns about high levels of coliform bacteria in the soaking tubs and a desire to revert the area to a more natural setting,

Area attractions: The overlook for Rainbow Falls is about 0.5 miles north of the hot spring on FR 1144. This waterfall cascades more than 100 feet, forming a brilliant rainbow when the sun hits it just right. A nice nearby day hike is the Shadow of the Sentinels trail. This gentle trail, located at Milepost 14 on the Baker Lake Road, features interpretive signs on the ecology and history of the area.

Carson Mineral Hot Springs Resort

Contact information:
Carson Mineral Hot Springs Resort
P.O. Box 1169
Carson, WA 98610
(509) 427–8292

General description: A sleepy Victorian-era hotel and bathhouse that features a regimen of therapeutic hot mineral baths reminiscent of old European spas.

Location: Washington Cascades, 50 miles east of Portland in the Columbia River Gorge.

Development: The hot springs have been developed commercially since the 1880s.

Best times to visit: Carson Resort is open year-round. The number of visitors can increase tenfold on the weekends, so come midweek if you want more solitude. The popularity of the cabins and hotel rooms makes it advisable to book reservations well in advance.

Restrictions: A fee is charged to use the individual soaking tubs and other facilities in the bathhouse. Men and women use different restricted areas of the bathhouse, and most bathe in the nude.

Access: Any vehicle can make the drive on the paved roads to the resort. The bathhouse is open from 8:00 A.M. to 7:30 P.M. in spring, summer, and fall. In winter the bathhouse hours are shortened to 9:00 A.M. to 6:00 P.M. on weekdays but stay open from 8:00 A.M. to 7:30 P.M. on weekends. Signs on the bathhouse entrance

Carson Mineral Hot Springs Resort

GIFFORD PINCHOT

NATIONAL FOREST

Wind

WIND

RIVER

RD

River

Shiperd
Falls

St. Martin
Springs Road

Carson Mineral
Hot Springs Resort

COLUMBIA RIVER GORGE

NATIONAL SCENIC AREA

Carson

HOT
SPRINGS
AVE

Dog
Mountain

W A S H I N G T O N

Columbia   River

14

Stevenson

30

COLUMBIA RIVER GORGE

To Hood River →

14

Cascade
Locks

84

NATIONAL SCENIC AREA

Wauna
Lake

Bonneville
Dam

Bridge
of the Gods

O R E G O N

← To Portland

COLUMBIA

N

WILDERNESS

Tomlike
Mountain

MOUNT HOOD

NATIONAL FOREST

0   Kilometers   5

0   Miles   5

caution pregnant women and visitors with heart problems to consult their physician before undergoing a soaking regimen.

Water temperature: The hot springs emerge from the banks of the Wind River at 136° F, and cool to around 126° F. by the time they reach the bathhouse. The soaking tubs can be adjusted to any comfortable bathing temperature.

Services: Some activities available at the resort include golfing on an 18-hole course, massage therapy, and treatment for poison ivy (which is common on the hillsides in the area). Groceries and gas are available in nearby Stevenson. The restaurant in the Hotel St. Martin serves breakfast, lunch, and dinner.

Accommodations: There are nine simple rooms in the hotel (with shared bathrooms down the hall) and twelve spartan cabins, each with a toilet and sink. The 1920s-era basic furnishings in each room and cabin include an iron bed, painted wooden dressers, and little else. A bit more upscale are two kitchenette suites, plus one deluxe suite with its own hot tub that can be filled with water from the natural hot springs. No television or phones are available in the rooms or cabins, which means guests usually go to bed early. Most visitors appreciate the quiet evenings in the little valley surrounding the resort. Camping and RV spots are also available near the cabins.

Map: Washington State Highway Map.

Finding the springs: From Portland drive east on I–84 along the Columbia River Gorge to Cascade Locks. Turn north and drive across the Bridge of the Gods into Washington. Drive east on WA 14 for 3 miles to Stevenson. Proceed east of Stevenson for 3.3 miles on WA 14, and turn left at the Carson Junction. Drive 1 mile to the center of the small town of Carson, and turn right at the four-way stop onto Hot Springs Avenue. Drive 1 mile east on Hot Springs Avenue. Turn left onto St. Martins Spring Road, next to the entrance to the golf course. You'll see a sign here pointing toward Carson Hot Springs. The St. Martin Springs Road takes a sharp drop for 0.5 mile to the resort. Drive past the cabins and bathhouse to the old hotel, and check in at the lobby for accommodations or passes for day soaking.

Overview: If you're looking for a luxurious spa treatment with elegantly furnished rooms, then Carson Mineral Hot Springs Resort isn't for you, but most visitors to this historic resort fall in love with the creaky Victorian-era hotel and the quirky hospital atmosphere of the bathhouse. With a prescribed, almost ritualistic approach, the resort follows the old European style of taking the mineral waters.

It's not a bad idea to make your reservation for a mineral-water treatment before you arrive. If you haven't done this, then schedule your mineral-bath ses-

Carson Hot Springs (also known as St. Martin's Hot Springs) in the early 1900s.
PHOTO: COURTESY OREGON HISTORICAL SOCIETY

sion when you check in at the front desk in the hotel. You'll receive a pass to give to the white-uniformed bath attendants when it's time for your session.

The bathhouse was built in 1923 and looks it. The wooden building is divided into separate men's and women's areas, each painted an institutional white. Both sides contain showers and a dressing area, a tiled tub room, and a body wrap room. The bathroom attendants (male on the men's side, female on the women's) will ask you to disrobe and hang your clothes on a hook (leave your valuables in your car trunk or hotel room). You'll then be taken to the tub room, which contains two rows of claw-foot, cast-iron tubs that have probably hosted thousands of bare bodies over the decades. The attendant will fill a tub with a mixture of hot mineral water and cooler spring water, usually settling for a mixed temperature of 101° to 104° F. (Individuals can increase or decrease the temperature as desired.) As you settle into the steamy water, the attendant will place a drinking cup under the hot water tap and recommend you drink the sulphurous water while you soak. (Years ago bathers were exhorted to consume up to five cups of the unpleasant-tasting hot spring water during their half-hour soak, but at present drinking any of the water is up to you.) You'll then be left alone to soak in and imbibe the hot water for a half hour. The tubs are so wide and deep that it's hard to keep from floating, but no one seems to mind.

After thirty minutes the attendant will return and prepare you for what the resort brochure calls "a warm, relaxing body wrap." Most visitors call it "the sweat treatment." The attendant will help you out of the soaking tub and will take you, still steaming and dripping, into the body-wrap room, which is filled with two dozen "sweat cots." Before your body cools down from the hot bath, you'll be wrapped in a thin flannel sheet, then laid on one of the padded wooden cots. The attendant will place thick cotton blankets on top of you, tucking them tightly around your sides and feet, then wrap your neck and head in thick towels, leaving only your face exposed.

In the 1940s guests would lie on the sweat cots in this mummified state for up to forty-five minutes. Current custom is to have you lie on the cot for about half an hour, which seems plenty. If you're claustrophobic, ask the attendant for a "loose wrap" to give your body a bit more room under the blankets, but longtime visitors ask for the "tight wrap" to build up a maximum sweat. No matter what the tightness of your wrap, in half an hour you'll be more than ready for a long cold shower. Most guests whimper their way back to their hotel room or cabin, where they sleep until dinner, then eat in the hotel restaurant to regain their strength in preparation for another regimen in the bathhouse the following day.

History: Isadore St. Martin discovered Carson Hot Springs in 1876 when he saw steam rising from the banks of the Wind River. St. Martin kept quiet about the existence of the hot springs until the land became available through the government; then he filed claim to homestead the property.

St. Martin's wife had been suffering from neuralgia, and St. Martin thought that she might benefit from bathing in the hot springs. He dug around the hot springs vent until he had made a hole large enough for his wife to bathe in. Mrs. St. Martin felt much better after these hot-water soaks, and soon word of the medicinal value of the hot springs spread to other people in the Columbia Gorge. An increasing number of visitors came to bathe in the thermal water, and St. Martin realized he could turn the hot springs into a commercial venture. At first he placed only a single soaking tub near the hot springs, but by 1900 he had built a large bathhouse near the river.

St. Martin envisioned a grand resort, complete with a hotel where guests could stay for a few days while they took therapeutic baths in the hot springs. He began building a three-story white clapboard hotel in 1897, completing the structure by 1900. The new hotel (which St. Martin named for himself) had twenty-four guest rooms, a large dining room, a kitchen, and a lobby. Supplies arrived at the resort by steamboat until the early 1900s, when the railroad began operation through the Columbia Gorge.

In 1907 a small bathhouse was built near the hotel, supplied with water piped 275 feet uphill from the riverside hot springs. Cold water from wooden barrels was ladled into each tub to adjust the temperature to individual tastes.

Isador St. Martin was proud of his new resort and of the beneficial properties of the hot springs, but he had little toleration for visitors who were critical of the almost miraculous cures that he ascribed to the hot water. This characteristic may have indirectly led to his untimely death. An article in the *County Pioneer* from March 17, 1910, recounts how St. Martin met his tragic fate:

Fatal Affair at Carson
Isador St. Martin Stabbed by Robert Brown During Quarrel.

[A visitor to the hot springs] . . . . had a quarrel about the quality of the water in St. Martin's Springs. This was always a sore spot with [Isador St. Martin], who, though he was of a quiet, industrious disposition, was always ready to scrap with anyone who made disparaging remarks about the quality of the water of these celebrated springs.

Old Man Brown made some disparaging remarks, which Mr. St. Martin wouldn't stand for, and had been ordered off the place. He was not going as fast as Mr. St. Martin thought he should, and Mr. St. Martin took him by the collar and started to push him along. When the old man struck backwards with a pocketknife, the blade penetrated just below the heart.

St. Martin died from the knife wound, but his heirs continued to run the resort for the next sixty-four years. Business flourished at the small resort, and in 1923 fourteen one-room cabins were built in a row above the road leading to the hotel. A larger bathhouse was constructed that same year, with separate wings for women and men. Massage rooms, soaking tubs, and rooms for sweat-cot treatments were included in the new bathhouse.

Local businessman Rudy Hegewald purchased the resort from St. Martin's heirs in 1974 and managed the hotel and other property for the next twenty years. In 1994 Hegewald sold the resort to Korean-based investor Gap Do Park for $3 million. The new owner announced his intentions to turn the sleepy resort into "the premier spa and resort in North America." Gap Park planned to invest $30 million to build a 200-room hotel, a 33,000-square-foot spa, and a 250-seat restaurant. Gap Park's plans have yet to be realized but are still being actively considered. For now the little hotel and bathhouse built by Isadore St. Martin operate much as they have for the past hundred years.

Area attractions: The Columbia Gorge Interpretive Center, near Stevenson, is a great place to spend an afternoon wandering through exhibits that detail the natural and cultural history along the Columbia River. Multnomah Falls, the second-highest year-round waterfall in the United States (and the most visited tourist site in Oregon), is located along I–84 just west of Cascade Locks on the Oregon side of Columbia Gorge. Nine miles north of Carson on Hemlock is the Forest Service's Wind River Information Center, which has lots of ideas for visiting area hiking trails and other waterfalls. The Upper Wind River Recreation Area is popular with cross-country skiers, snowmobilers, and snowshoe aficionados.

Soap Lake

Contact information:
Soap Lake Chamber of Commerce
P.O. Box 433
Soap Lake, WA 98851
(509) 246–1821
www.soaplakecoc.org

Soap Lake Conservancy
P.O. Box 65
Soap Lake, WA 98851
(509) 766–1699
www.thelake.org

General description: A small spa town on the banks of a mineral-rich lake that has attracted health seekers since the late 1800s.

Location: Central Washington, 120 miles west of Spokane, 180 miles east of Seattle.

Development: The first homesteader arrived on the shores of Soap Lake in 1901. By the time the town of Soap Lake was incorporated in 1919, it already had four hotels and several rooming houses. Many of the elegant hotels and sanitariums are now gone, but the town still hosts visitors from around the world who seek the benefits of the alkaline lake.

Best times to visit: The warm months of July, August, and September are best if you want to swim in Soap Lake or bake in the sunshine while taking a mud bath. The town hosts a popular Fourth of July celebration (check the Soap Lake Chamber of Commerce Web site for scheduled events). The cooler months of the year are much less crowded than the summer—bathing in the lake drops off dramatically after Labor Day. Winter visitors usually stay in one of the motels supplied with heated mineral water.

Restrictions: Swimsuits are required on Soap Lake's municipal beaches.

Access: Soap Lake is located on WA 17. Any vehicle can make the trip.

Water temperature: There's no thermal source heating the mineral water in Soap Lake, so the water temperature fluctuates with the seasons. The warmest

Soap Lake

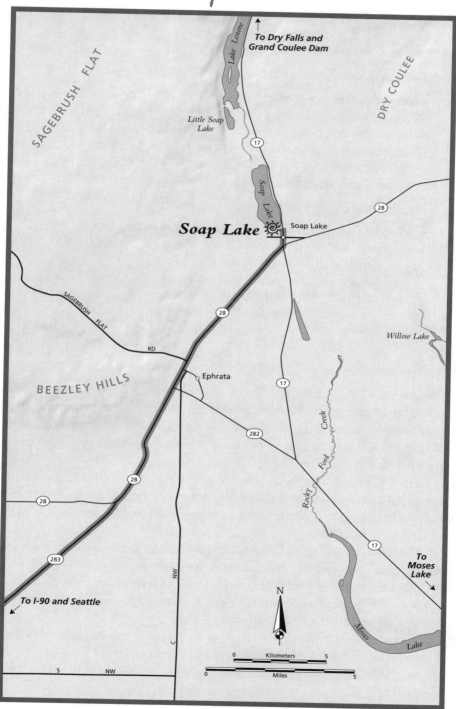

To Dry Falls and
Grand Coulee Dam

DRY COULEE

SAGEBRUSH FLAT

Lake Lenore

Little Soap
Lake

17

Soap Lake

Soap Lake Soap Lake

28

SAGEBRUSH FLAT

Willow Lake

RD

BEEZLEY HILLS

Ephrata

28

17

282

Rocky Ford Creek

28

28

283

To I-90 and Seattle

NW

C

17

To
Moses
Lake

N

Moses Lake

0 Kilometers 5

0 Miles 5

5 NW

lake temperature occurs in late summer, when the shallow lake can exceed 80° F. The lake water is piped to several motels and other businesses in town. More than 40 percent of the buildings in Soap Lake have dual water systems, one with fresh water and one with mineralized lake water. The mineral water is usually heated before it's used in showers and hot tubs.

Services: Groceries, gas, food, and lodging are all available in Soap Lake.

Accommodations: The town of Soap Lake has close to a dozen inns, motels, and resorts. Two of the best-known lodging options are the Inn at Soap Lake and Notaras Lodge, both located a short walk from the lakeshore. Other motels in town that have mineral-water baths and showers include the Lake Motel, Royal View Motel, and Tolo Vista Motel. The Smokiam RV Campground, located on Soap Lake's East Beach, features forty-eight RV sites and four tent campsites.

Map: Washington State Highway Map.

Finding the lake: From Spokane drive 100 miles west on I–90 to exit 179 (Moses Lake/Ephrata exit). Drive north on WA 17 for 24 miles to Ephrata. Continue on WA 17 north for another 4 miles to Soap Lake.

From Seattle drive 150 miles east on I–90 to exit 151. Take WA 283 north for 15 miles, until the highway turns into WA 28. Continue north on WA 28 for 11 miles to Ephrata. From Ephrata take WA 17 4 miles north to Soap Lake.

Overview: Soap Lake is a highly alkaline body of water that has no natural inlet. Coming from springs far beneath its surface, the lake's water passes through highly mineralized rock. The unique mineral component in the brackish water and bottom mud is the source of the healing properties sought by visitors to the little town on the lakeshore.

Summer bathers have their choice of two public beaches: East Beach is the most popular, with a snack bar, large beachfront, campground, and excellent views; bathers seeking solitude away from the city center gather at the more secluded West Beach.

Over the years several techniques have evolved for health seekers to use the mineral waters. A public fountain on Main Street allows visitors to fill gallon jugs with either the freshwater or the mineral-rich water from Soap Lake. Some visitors return every summer to Soap Lake and pack their car trunks with dozens of gallon containers filled with the salty-tasting water.

Floating and swimming in the brackish water during summer is another popular way to enjoy Soap Lake. Brightly colored copepods (small shrimplike crustaceans) glitter in the sunshine in the lake, which is too salty to support any freshwater fish.

Mud baths are a third common vehicle for benefiting from the minerals found in the lake. Soap Lake contains deposits of both olive-green and deep-black mud, and locals treasure secret locations of their favorite mud, much like prospectors who hide the location of gold strikes. During the annual Fourth of July celebration, the lakeshore is lined with visitors who wait patiently to be coated with gooey mud by city volunteers. The slime-covered guests then bake in the sun until the mud dries to a crusty shell. A quick swim in the waters of Soap Lake then removes the mud.

History: In 1811 six Hudson's Bay Company trappers observed Native Americans from the Cayuse tribe taking steam baths in huts on the shores of Soap Lake. The Cayuse called the lake *Smokiam,* meaning "healing waters." They would heat a pile of rocks in a fire, then splash the rocks with lake water to create steam in the huts. Settlers in the late 1800s gave the lake its current name when they observed the frothy, soapy bubbles that whipped up around the lakeshore after a strong wind.

Like the Cayuse tribe before them, the early cowboys were aware of the healing properties of the water of Soap Lake. Many tales were told of the miraculous cures realized by early pioneers who drank and bathed in the water. Some of these stories were pretty far-fetched. One cowboy legend concerning Soap Lake was described in the *Grant County Journal* in May 15, 1908:

Friends enjoying a mud bath at Soap Lake.

In the early days, a band of cowboys were camped near the lake, when one of their members died. His mates buried him near the shoreline and rode on down the range another 50 miles. Two weeks later the boys were surprised to see their comrade (deceased) ride into the camp on a Cayuse [horse] he had picked up on the range. He said that he had been dead alright, but the water of the lake had seeped through until it had reached his body and brought him back to life.

Another story of Soap Lake's miraculous properties appeared in the same article:

Tony Richardson told us that a man was then stopping at the [Soap Lake] hotel who came 40 days before without hair on his head, and now his hair is two inches long.

A little over a decade later the *Wenatchee Daily World* published the following two accounts of the healing properties of Soap Lake:

A well-known resident of Wenatchee, whose name can be furnished by inquiries, barely avoided an operation for appendicitis, which his physician insisted was the seat of his trouble. He instead came to Soap Lake, and after drinking the lake water expelled a tapeworm 36 feet in length and went home completely restored to health.

This story was also reported in the *Wenatchee Daily World*:

An old Swede from Spokane, 75 years old, was scabby all over with eczema, and was getting quite blind and had to quit work. He was put in the mud baths, and with only his nose sticking out, and commenced to sing, saying he was in heaven, and had not been free of pain for years until then. He was cured after taking 30 baths.

Rattlesnake bites were not uncommon in eastern Washington, and Soap Lake was known for its ability to treat victims of the venomous vipers. In May of 1929 the *Grant County Journal* carried this letter to the editor about such a treatment:

To whom it may concern: After suffering from the after effects of a rattlesnake bite of a year and one half standing, in the form of stiffened muscles and joints, partial loss of use of one leg, blood destruction and heart trouble, and going everywhere for healing and health, the Mayo brothers advised a trip to Soap Lake as a possible place of relief.

With the use of a cane I was able to slowly, and painfully, walk. After six weeks of Soap Lake treatment, I am able to walk as good as ever, and my other troubles are almost gone. There is no question in my mind but that Soap Lake water has curative powers that cannot be found elsewhere, and I offer this testimony from a fair and impartial view, as it looks to me.

Signed,
C.L. Nevins, DDS, LeMars, Iowa.

As the town became more cosmopolitan, some of the local customs had to be changed. A history produced by the Soap Lake Chamber of Commerce recalled one of these changes:

Guns were finally outlawed in town because of the danger to swimmers caused by fun-seekers who sat on the shore and took pot shots at low flying birds over the water. The pistol packers were unhappy about being deprived of their evening entertainment, and argued that the birds were nuisances anyway.

Soap Lake flourished as a destination resort in the early 1900s, until several tragedies struck in the 1920s, when three of the largest hotels in town burned to the ground. The Great Depression in the early 1930s hit the tourist trade hard, and a long drought dealt a further blow to the economy of the area. The construction of the Grand Coulee Dam in the 1940s helped revitalize the spa town, although it never returned to its status as one of the most popular destination resorts in Eastern Washington. Presently Soap Lake is a quiet outpost halfway between Seattle and Spokane. The past decade has seen an increase in new residents, primarily retirees and persons seeking to escape the pressures of urban life.

Area attractions: Soap Lake is a great base to use to investigate many of the attractions of central Washington. A half-hour drive north of Soap Lake is the Grand Coulee Dam, the biggest concrete dam in the world. During evenings in July, August, and September, what's billed as "the world's largest laser light show" plays across the wide expanse of the dam.

Between Soap Lake and Grand Coulee Dam is the Dry Falls Dam Visitor Center, which explains the story behind what may have been the largest waterfall in history. More than 13,000 years ago, a gigantic glacial flood roared through central Washington. The overlook at Dry Falls provides a great view of the site where the waterfall, 400 feet tall and more than 3.5 miles wide, formed during the flood. Sun Lakes State Park, located a few miles from the Dry Falls Visitor Center, features camping sites, cabins, hiking, horseback riding, swimming, and golf.

Oregon Hot Springs

Bagby Hot Springs

Contact information:
Estacada Ranger District
595 Northwest Industrial Way
Estacada, OR 97023
(503) 630–6861

Friends of Bagby Hot Springs
P.O. Box 1798
Clackamas, OR 97015-1798
www.bagbyhotsprings.org

General description: A well-known backcountry soaking site nestled in a grove of old-growth cedar and Douglas fir. Hand-hewn log bathtubs filled with steaming hot water attract diverse crowds.

Location: Oregon Cascades, 65 miles southeast of Portland in Mount Hood National Forest.

Development: Semideveloped. Over the past twenty years, volunteers with the Friends of Bagby Hot Springs have constructed rustic bathhouses and hot tubs, but the surrounding old-growth forest still lends the area a wilderness feel.

Best times to visit: With downtown Portland less than a two-hour drive from its trailhead, Bagby is one of the most popular hot springs in the Oregon Cascades. Weekends and holidays are particularly busy, and it's not uncommon to wait for an hour or so for your turn in the soaking tubs. Once the sun sets Bagby can get rowdy—families might want to leave the area before dark. (The USFS has recently stepped up patrols at Bagby and hopes to calm the party atmosphere.) You'll rarely find any time of the year when you'll have the hot springs to yourself. Try visiting in midweek in the morning or on rainy or colder winter days to beat the crowds.

Restrictions: The hot springs are open twenty-four hours a day, 365 days a year. A Northwest Forest Pass is required to park at the trailhead and to use the hot springs. Purchase your pass at the Estacada Ranger Station on your way to the hot springs if you don't already have one ($5.00 for a day pass and $30.00 for an

Bagby Hot Springs

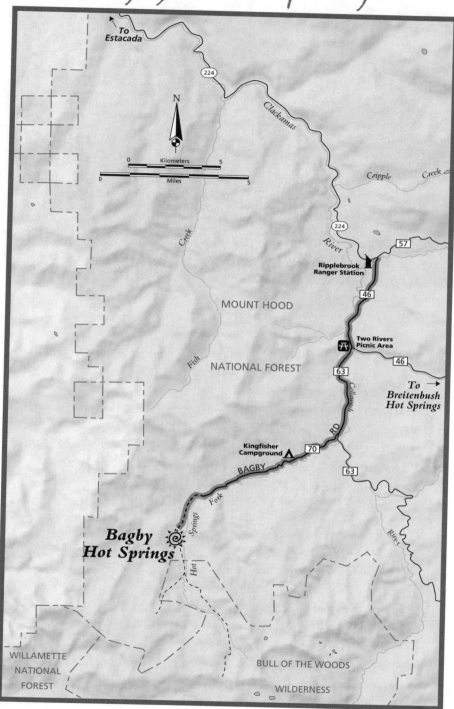

To
Estacada

224

N

Kilometers
0   5

Miles
0   5

Clackamas

Cripple   Creek

224

57

River

Ripplebrook
Ranger Station

46

MOUNT HOOD

Two Rivers
Picnic Area

NATIONAL FOREST

63   46

To
Breitenbush
Hot Springs

Collawash

Kingfisher
Campground   70   RD

BAGBY   63

Fork

Bagby
Hot Springs   Springs

Hot   River

WILLAMETTE
NATIONAL   BULL OF THE WOODS

FOREST   WILDERNESS

Fish   Creek

A rustic bathhouse at Bagby Hot Springs.

annual pass). You can also obtain a Northwest Forest Pass at any other USFS office or in many outdoor supply stores. No campfires or overnight camping are allowed at the hot springs. Nudity is permitted in the soaking-tub area, but not in the open areas surrounding the bathhouses. Since the trail to the hot springs is also a gateway trail into the Bull of the Mountains Wilderness, motorized vehicles and mountain bikes are prohibited.

Access: Most of the year any vehicle can make the trip on the paved roads that lead to Bagby, although winter snows sometimes block the final few miles. After a snowstorm it's not unusual to see an abandoned car stuck in snow on the road to the Bagby trailhead. (Call the Estacada Ranger District to check on road conditions in winter.) Backcountry skiers delight in visiting Bagby when the snows dissuade the usual crowds. Skiing distance from the road can exceed 10 miles one way, depending on how far up you can drive on FR 70 before snowdrifts force you to park your car and strap on your skis.

Water temperature: The two hot springs that feed the hot tubs and bathhouses flow out of the ground at 136° F. Cold water can be added to the tubs to cool them to a comfortable soaking temperature.

Services: No services are available on site except for a pit toilet. Be sure to bring plenty of drinking water, as none is available at the hot springs.

Accommodations: To preserve the solitude of the hot springs, camping is not allowed near the soaking areas. Tent sites are available 0.25 mile beyond the hot springs along the Hot Springs Fork of the Collawash River. Backpackers stopping to soak at the springs sometimes continue another 7 miles south past the hot springs to Silver King Lake in the Bull of the Woods Wilderness. Another overnight option is Kingfisher Campground, which is maintained by the USFS about 4 miles east of the Bagby parking area on FR 70.

Maps: Oregon State Highway Map, USFS Mount Hood National Forest map.

Finding the springs: From Portland drive south on I–205 to exit 9 (the Estacada Exit). Drive east on OR 224 for 18 miles to Estacada. Stop at the Estacada Ranger Station to get the latest information on the road conditions and hot springs trail and to purchase a Northwest Forest Pass if you don't already have one. From Estacada drive 25 miles east on OR 224 to the Ripplebrook Ranger Station. About 0.5 mile east of Ripplebrook, turn south at the Timothy Lake Junction onto FR 46. Head south on FR 46 for 3 miles to FR 63. Take FR 63 south for 4 miles; then turn right (southwest) onto FR 70. Drive 6 miles southwest on FR 70 to the parking area for Bagby Hot Springs.

Another scenic way to get to Bagby is to drive east from Salem to Detroit along OR 22. From Detroit head north on paved FR 46, past Breitenbush Hot Springs and down the Clackamas River to the Two Rivers Picnic Area at the intersection with FR 63. Turn south on FR 63, drive 6.1 miles to FR 70, and then turn southwest for 2.8 miles to the Bagby Hot Springs parking area. This route from Detroit is often closed in winter.

The parking area at the Bagby trailhead is infamous for vandalism, and you'll likely see several piles of broken windshield glass on the ground that testify to auto break-ins. Forest Service patrols have been stepped up over the last few years to help reduce car vandalism (called "car clouting" in Forest Service brochures), but in spite of increased patrols, the vandalism is still a serious problem. It's best to leave all your valuables at home; if this isn't possible, at least place them in your trunk or pack them with you to the hot springs.

The trail to the hot springs is located just behind the information sign in the parking area. Allow thirty to forty-five minutes to hike the 1.5 miles to the hot springs. For the most part it's a gentle hike on a well-maintained trail, but the last 0.25 mile is a bit steep. Pack a flashlight in your daypack—you'll need it to help you find your way back down the trail through the pitch-black, old-growth forest if you are hiking to your car after dusk.

Overview: Ask most hot springs veterans to name their favorite soaking spot in Oregon, and Bagby is sure to come out near the top of their lists. The handcrafted

One of the wooden hot tubs at Bagby Hot Springs.

rustic cedar bathhouses and soaking tubs seem designed more for hobbits and trolls than for weekend baby boomers from Portland.

There are three soaking areas surrounding the historic ranger cabin at Bagby. The community hot tub at the upper bathhouse is a spacious 6 feet in diameter and 4 feet deep. The tub holds six to eight people, and local custom is to invite newcomers to join those already in the hot tub. A wooden flume passes by the hot tub, carrying water from the 136° F. upper hot springs. A rubber ball the size of a grapefruit can be lowered into the flume, which will divert the hot water stream into the hot tub (you'll figure it out once you see the flume). It takes about thirty minutes to fill the hot tub. There's also a valve that allows cold water from the nearby stream to mix with the steaming hot water in the tub. While you wait for the tub to fill with hot water, peruse the carved initials left by previous bathers on the sides of the hot tub.

A second 136° F. hot spring flows out of a rock fissure about 30 yards uphill from the two lower bathhouses. This hot spring flows for several yards through a channel cut in the surrounding rock, until it is collected by a second wooden flume. This flume is attached to the back of the lower bathhouses, on the opposite side of the bathhouse wall from the tubs. The newest bathhouse consists of five private tub rooms, each containing a hand-hewn 10-foot by 3-foot tub made from a cedar log. There's a cleverly-designed wooden baffle next to a spout in the wall of each private tub room that connects to the hot-water flume. Lowering the baffle diverts hot spring water from the flume into the tub. A cedar roof covers half of each tub, leaving half exposed to the elements. If it's raining, you can orient yourself in the tub to keep your head covered under the roof, while your toes can wiggle in the raindrops.

The third bathhouse contains three of the original cedar tubs from Bagby's original bathhouse, as well as a large circular hot tub. There aren't any private rooms in this bathhouse, so if you want privacy, you'll need to wait for one of the private tub rooms to open up in the newest bathhouse.

Between the two bathhouses lies a large wooden cistern that's filled with cold water from the nearby stream. Ten-gallon buckets are provided to haul water from the cistern to the tubs to cool them to a comfortable temperature (it usually takes several buckets to cool the water enough for bathing). After you've finished soaking at Bagby, take one of the large brushes located nearby to scrub down your tub for the next bather.

History: A prospector named Robert W. Bagby discovered the hot springs in 1881. Bagby apparently did little to develop the hot springs other than lend them his name. In 1913 a log cabin was built near the hot springs, which was used as a Forest Service ranger station through the 1940s. (The cabin is currently on the National Register of Historic Places.) In 1939 the Civilian Conservation Corps built the first bathhouse at Bagby. The bathhouse featured five separate rooms, each containing a rustic bathtub carved out of a large cedar log.

Early visitors to the hot springs used mules to carry their gear on the three-day trek that followed winding forest trails. Because of its isolation, the hot springs received few visitors during the eighty years following Robert Bagby's first visit to the area. In 1960 the solitude was shattered when a new logging road allowed visitors to drive within a couple of miles of the hot springs. The popularity of the rustic location boomed, and weekends often saw several hundred visitors to the springs. The USFS stationed a full-time ranger at the springs to oversee the crowds during these years.

In 1979 the original bathhouse was destroyed by fire. Many people suspected that a bather had left a candle burning in one of the tub rooms, which set the cedar-walled bathhouse ablaze. A local volunteer group called the Friends of Bagby Hot Springs was formed in the early 1980s to rebuild the bathhouse, and they also acquired a lease from the USFS to help manage the hot springs area. In 1983 this volunteer group built a hot tub near the upper hot springs and a year later constructed a bathhouse at the lower hot springs. Three of the original cedar tubs salvaged from the ashes of the original bathhouse were placed in the lower-springs bathhouse, along with a new hot tub. The third bathhouse (still called the "New Bathhouse") was built adjacent to the lower-springs bathhouse in 1985 and was outfitted with five new log tubs.

In the fall of 2001, management disagreements with the USFS led to the termination of the lease with the Friends of Bagby Hot Springs. Some members of the volunteer group hope to reestablish a partnership with the USFS to help manage the area in the future, but whether this will happen has yet to be seen.

Area attractions: Kayakers and rafters enjoy the challenging water on the nearby Clackamas River. The Bagby trailhead is a major gateway to the Bull of the Woods Wilderness Area. The Table Rock Wilderness, Salmon Huckleberry Wilderness, and the Olallie Lake Scenic Area are all located within an easy drive from Bagby.

Breitenbush Hot Springs Retreat and Conference Center

Contact information:
Breitenbush Hot Springs Retreat and Conference Center
P.O. Box 578
Detroit, OR 97342
(503) 854–3314
www.breitenbush.com

General description: A worker-owned cooperative and intentional community situated in an old-growth forest, offering personal-growth retreats and group workshops. More than a half dozen hot springs pools and a natural sauna are available to retreat guests and day visitors.

Location: Oregon Cascades, 60 miles east of Salem.

Development: Breitenbush features rustic soaking pools in a mountain meadow, tiled soaking tubs near the Breitenbush River, and a log-cabin sauna heated by natural hot springs. A central lodge and dining room, gift shop and registration office, meditation center, and guest cabins are located on the property.

Best times to visit: Workshops and retreats are held throughout the year, most of them available to the public (check the Breitenbush Web site or request a copy of their quarterly catalog for the list of future events). Breitenbush is busiest during the week of summer solstice (late June), when several hundred visitors gather to celebrate shared community and spiritual renewal. Certain weeks during the year are reserved for registered workshop participants.

Breitenbush Hot Springs Retreat and Conference Center

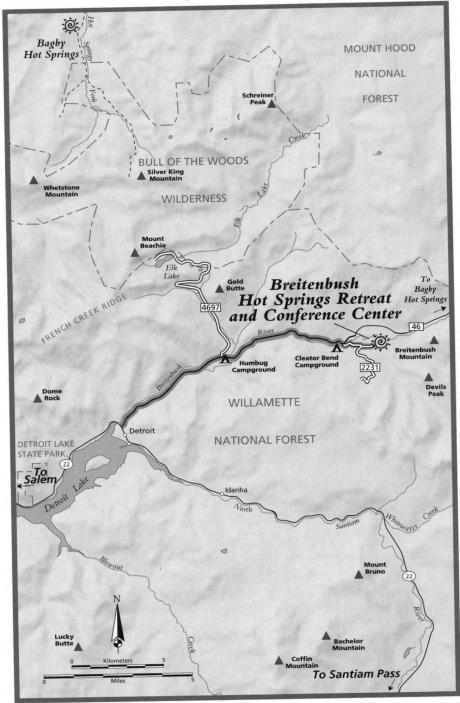

Bagby Hot Springs

MOUNT HOOD

NATIONAL

FOREST

Hot Springs Fork

Schreiner Peak

BULL OF THE WOODS

Silver King Mountain

WILDERNESS

Whetstone Mountain

Elk Lake Creek

Mount Beachie

Elk Lake

Gold Butte

French Creek Ridge

4697

Breitenbush Hot Springs Retreat and Conference Center

To Bagby Hot Springs

46

River

Humbug Campground

Cleator Bend Campground

2231

Breitenbush Mountain

Breitenbush

Dome Rock

Devils Peak

WILLAMETTE

Detroit

NATIONAL FOREST

DETROIT LAKE STATE PARK

22

To Salem

Detroit Lake

Idanha

North Santiam

Whitewater Creek

Blowout

Mount Bruno

22

River

N

Lucky Butte

Coffin Mountain

Bachelor Mountain

To Santiam Pass

Kilometers

Miles

0   5

0   5

Creek

Restrictions: Day visitors are welcome to use the thermal pools and sauna from 9:00 A.M. to 6:00 P.M. (reservations required). Workshop participants and overnight guests can use the hot springs pools and sauna twenty-four hours a day. Nudity is the norm in the soaking pools and sauna, though the rest of the resort is not clothing-optional. The retreat does not permit alcohol, electrical appliances, glass containers, candles, incense, or pets. Smoking is allowed only in designated outdoor areas.

Access: Any vehicle can drive to Breitenbush on the paved and gravel roads leading to the retreat center.

Water temperature: The maximum measured surface temperature at the five dozen natural thermal springs is 198° F. The meadow soaking pools are maintained between 100° and 105° F. The four hot tubs near the river vary from 103° to 112° F, and a fifth cold-water plunge rarely exceeds 60° F.

Services: Three vegetarian meals are served each day in the main lodge. Free well-being classes are offered two to six times daily, including yoga, meditation, and chanting. Trained therapists offer massage, hydrotherapy, and Reiki sessions.

Accommodations: Lodging at Breitenbush is centered around forty-two guest cabins, some with private toilets and sinks. A common bathhouse with separate men's and women's showers is available near the cabins. All cabins are geothermally heated. Bring your own sleeping bags, blankets, pillows, and towels. Tent camping is allowed during the popular solstice healing retreats, when cabins are given preferentially to families with young children.

If you're on a budget and want cheaper overnight accommodations, consider camping at nearby Cleator Bend or Humbug Forest Service Campgrounds on FR 46. You can then pay a day-use fee to use the Breitenbush hot springs and sauna.

Map: Oregon State Highway Map.

Finding the springs: From Salem, head east on OR 22 for 50 miles to the town of Detroit (at the edge of the Detroit reservoir). Turn north at the gas station in Detroit onto FR 46. Drive 10 miles north. Just past the Cleator Bend Campground, turn right onto a single-lane bridge across the Breitenbush River. Drive 1.5 miles on this gravel road (FR 2231) to the Breitenbush parking lot. The parking lot was purposely built several hundred yards from the cabins, lodge, and hot springs to isolate the sounds of automobiles from the serenity of the resort. Cleverly designed handcarts are available in the parking lot to help accommodate the transport of your luggage. Register at the main office building to get directions to your cabin.

If you are driving from Portland, an alternate route to Breitenbush is to take OR 244 from Portland through Estacada to the Ripplebrook Guard Station and then continue on paved FR 46 to Breitenbush. This road is not maintained for winter travel and may be impassable from November through March.

Overview: Breitenbush Hot Springs Retreat and Conference Center is a great place to get away from urban pressures for a few days of reflection, relaxation, and renewal. The center is known in the Pacific Northwest for its emphasis on holistic living and personal wellness. Breitenbush encourages guests to be proactive in their own well-being and offers dozens of workshops and retreats throughout the year on such topics as conflict resolutions in relationships, meditation, yoga, and rhythm and dance.

A sign by the bubbling "Magic Pool" near the main lodge claims that Breitenbush Hot Springs is the largest thermal springs area in the Oregon Cascades. Approximately sixty thermal springs and seeps occur on the hillsides and river valley near the resort, with an aggregate flow of 900 gallons per minute. The hottest thermal springs have a recorded temperature of 198° F.

There are three separate areas where you can enjoy the thermal waters at Breitenbush. The meadow pools overlook the Breitenbush River, providing the most dramatic view of the surrounding mountains. At night these pools provide a wonderful opportunity for stargazing.

Relaxing in the meadow pool at Breitenbush Hot Springs.

The biggest of the meadow pools is known as the "Sacred Pool," which measures 12 by 20 feet and is 2 to 3 feet deep. This pool often has a no-talking rule in effect to allow guests to soak in silence. Two smaller pools lie against the treeline between the Sacred Pool and the Main Lodge. The temperature of the meadow pools hovers around 105° F.

Adjacent to the main lodge is an old cedar steam sauna. A natural hot-water stream flows beneath the sauna, providing steamy heat to the dark wood interior of the building.

The Medicine Wheel Hot Tubs compose the third soaking area at Breitenbush. The hot tubs are aligned with the four points of the compass and honor the four seasons. A cold-water tub provides welcome relief from long, hot soaks. The hot tubs are cleaned three times a day while guests are eating meals in the main lodge.

History: Breitenbush Hot Springs and the Breitenbush River were named for Peter Breitenbush, a one-armed Dutchman who settled at the mouth of the river in the 1840s. Hunters and trappers frequented the area through the 1800s. In July of 1887 John Waldo of Salem visited the undeveloped hot springs. Waldo was suffering from an illness and reported that the mineral water had alleviated his condition:

> The water is helping me and could not well do otherwise if there is any virtue in it, for I sit for two hours of a morning snuffing it through a tube.

In 1893 Waldo again returned to the hot springs and reported on the new buildings constructed for persons seeking the medicinal benefits of the hot water:

> A log bath house, very plain, had been built over one of the hot springs, with a rather narrow cedar tub and a platform directly over the spring for a steam bath. Hot water is dipped out of the springs and cold water carried up from under the bank to temper it, and closing the door the steam from the spring makes a very agreeable chamber to bathe in. We all took a bath and pronounced it excellent.

In 1904 a settler named Mansfield applied for a homestead to the hot springs and surrounding land, selling it a few years later to a corporation. The corporation built tent platforms near the springs to provide sleeping quarters for summer visitors. In autumn the tents were removed from the platforms, and the area was abandoned until the deep winter snows melted the following spring.

Merle Bruckman purchased the hot springs in 1927. Bruckman's father had developed the technique for making ice-cream cones and had become wealthy

The mineral springs bathhouse and pool at Breitenbush Hot Springs in 1933.

after the new dessert was introduced at the St. Louis World's Fair in 1904. The twenty-seven-year-old Bruckman wanted to invest some of the family wealth in building a wilderness resort, and Breitenbush Hot Springs seemed perfect for his vision.

By 1930 Bruckman had built a 100-foot-by-40-foot swimming pool, a bathhouse, guest cabins, and a hydroelectric generator. He began advertising the little resort as "Bruckman's Breitenbush Mineral Springs." Over the next few years, he added a gas station, a main lodge with thirty-two guest rooms, a grocery store, a post office, a soda fountain, a restaurant, and a dance hall. The resort flourished for two decades under Bruckman's management.

In the mid-1950s Bruckman sold the property, and the resort soon began to decline. The property passed through a series of owners and finally closed to the public in 1972. For five years it sat abandoned, surrounded by barbed wire and NO TRESPASSING signs.

In 1977, fifty years after young Merle Bruckman had first developed Breitenbush into a resort, another twenty-seven-year-old bought the property. Alex Beamer from Oakland, California, had been involved with self-sufficiency and spirituality for several years and was seeking a location to establish a personal-growth center. Beamer purchased the abandoned property for $250,000, using $100,000 of a family inheritance and borrowing the rest of the money.

Within three years Beamer and the volunteers who supported his vision had brought the little resort back up to code and had acquired a commercial business license. In 1985 Beamer sold his ownership to a newly formed cooperative that supported his ideals of a self-sufficient community built around personal growth. For the past fifteen years, Breitenbush has been managed as a worker-owned and worker-administrated cooperative corporation.

Area attractions: More than 20 miles of hiking trails lead from the hot springs into the surrounding old-growth forest. During winter Breitenbush offers cross-country ski weekends into the Mount Jefferson Wilderness, about 10 miles from the resort. In the summer months Bagby Hot Springs can be reached by driving north on FR 46 through the Clackamas River Valley.

9

Deer Creek (Bigelow) Hot Springs

Contact information:
McKenzie Ranger District
57600 McKenzie Highway
McKenzie Bridge, OR 97413
(541) 822–3317

General description: A warm soaking pool in a fern-lined grotto on the banks of the McKenzie River.

Location: Oregon Cascades, 61 miles east of Eugene in the McKenzie River Valley.

Development: Undeveloped, except for the crude dam of rocks that slows the influx of cold river water into the grotto.

Best times to visit: You are most likely to find a warm soak at Deer Creek Hot Springs when the river level in the McKenzie is low (late summer through winter). During spring runoff, cold river water can wash out the hot springs. Summer visits are preferable, as the soaking temperature is rather tepid. Weekdays are less crowded than weekends or holidays.

Restrictions: The hot springs are restricted to daytime use only. Swimsuits are optional.

Access: Any vehicle can make the trip up OR 126 and the paved forest road to the parking area.

Water temperature: A sluggish flow of hot water emerges from the grotto at around 130° F, but the soaking pool itself averages 85° to 100° F. The pool temperature can become quite chilly in spring, when the cold water from the

Deer Creek (Bigelow) Hot Springs

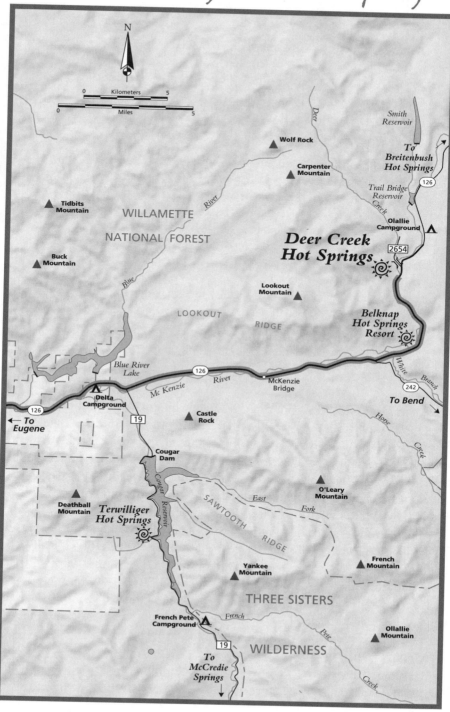

N

Kilometers 5
0

Miles 5
0

Smith
Reservoir

Wolf Rock

To
Breitenbush
Hot Springs

Carpenter
Mountain

Trail Bridge
Reservoir

126

Tidbits
Mountain

WILLAMETTE

Olallie
Campground

NATIONAL FOREST

Deer Creek
Hot Springs

2654

Buck
Mountain

Lookout
Mountain

Belknap
Hot Springs
Resort

LOOKOUT

RIDGE

Blue River
Lake

126

Blue River

Mc Kenzie River

McKenzie
Bridge

White Branch

242

Delta
Campground

To Bend

126

To
Eugene

19

Castle
Rock

Horse Creek

Cougar
Dam

Deathball
Mountain

Terwilliger
Hot Springs

Canyon Reservoir

SAWTOOTH

East Fork

O'Leary
Mountain

RIDGE

Yankee
Mountain

French
Mountain

THREE SISTERS

French Pete
Campground

French

Ollallie
Mountain

19

WILDERNESS

To
McCredie
Springs

Pete Creek

McKenzie River washes over the crude dam of river rocks that enclose the soaking pool.

Services: None available at the springs.

Accommodations: Olallie Campground is located 1.5 miles northeast of the hot springs just off OR 126. More comfortable lodging is available at Belknap Hot Springs, 4.2 miles to the southeast. Belknap offers river-view rooms in its main lodge, as well as cabins with kitchen facilities, a camping area, and several dozen hookups for RVs.

Map: Oregon State Highway Map.

Finding the springs: From Eugene drive 53 miles east on OR 126 to the town of McKenzie Bridge. Proceed another 8 miles east on OR 126, and turn left onto FR 2654 (located between highway mile markers 14 and 15). Drive on FR 2654 for 0.1 mile, and cross the Deer Creek Bridge spanning the McKenzie River. Immediately after crossing the bridge, turn right into a small parking area. Lock your car and walk across the road toward the bridge. Both the popular McKenzie River Trail and a lesser-used footpath to Deer Creek Hot Springs parallel the McKenzie River. The McKenzie River Trail heads uphill—don't take this route. Instead look for Deer Creek Hot Springs day-use sign next to the bridge. The trail you want to take can be seen along the riverbank just behind the sign. Follow this trail downstream for about 100 yards to the hot springs.

Overview: Deer Creek Hot Springs is a mellow little soaking pool on the upper stretches of the McKenzie River. The hot springs are also known as Bigelow Hot Springs and McKenzie River Hot Springs, although the Forest Service has settled on Deer Creek Hot Springs as its official name. The hot springs are less popular than the larger (and hotter) soaking venues in the Oregon Cascades such as McCredie, Bagby, and Terwilliger, but they're still worth visiting if you're driving through the McKenzie River Valley.

There's only one soaking pool at Deer Creek Hot Springs, but it's a beauty. The 8-foot by 12-foot pool sits a few feet from the McKenzie River. Half of the pool is enclosed by a 4-foot-deep grotto covered with ferns and moss. You can choose to sit inside the grotto (where the water tends to be a bit warmer) or soak in the exposed portion of the pool with a better view of the McKenzie River. Keep your eyes peeled for water ouzels bobbing and chirping on the rocks in the river current. These small brown birds actually fly underwater for short distances, searching for small insects.

Rainwater and condensed mist from the hot springs collect in the ferns on the roof of the grotto, causing a gentle sprinkle of cold-water droplets on the bathers

The fern-covered grotto at Deer Creek Hot Springs.

below. The bottom of the soaking pool is covered with a layer of fine silt, which muddies the pool water when disturbed. The soaking pool can comfortably hold four or more. When the river level is low, the soaking pool can reach temperatures over 100° F. Usually the pool temperature is a few degrees cooler, and you may find the pool washed out completely during spring runoff. The highway is barely visible through the trees on the opposite site of the river, but road warriors can't see the bathers. Nudity is common, though no one seems to care if his or her fellow bathers are wearing a swimsuit or soaking in the buff.

Area attractions: The McKenzie River Trail passes on the ridge a few yards behind Deer Creek Hot Springs. This hiking trail starts at Clear Lake and passes several scenic waterfalls as it parallels the McKenzie River for more than 30 miles. There are close to a dozen entrance points to the hiking trail along Oregon Highway 126, and weekend visitors often hike short sections of the trail. Whitewater rafting and fishing are popular recreational activities on the river. Winter visitors enjoy cross-country skiing on the hiking trails. Downhill skiers gather at Hoodoo Ski Bowl on Santiam Pass, 20 miles east of Deer Creek Hot Springs.

Belknap Hot Springs Resort

Contact information:
Belknap Hot Springs Resort
59296 Belknap Springs Road
P.O. Box 2001
McKenzie Bridge, OR 97413
(541) 882–3512

General description: A well-known commercial resort on the banks of the McKenzie River.

Location: Oregon Cascades, 55 miles east of Eugene.

Development: Belknap has been commercially developed for more than a century. Current facilities include two warm-water pools, a main lodge, rental cabins, and RV and camping spots.

Best times to visit: The resort is popular year-round. Rafting guides rendezvous with their clients in the Belknap Lodge before floating the McKenzie River in the spring and summer months; hunters pack the RV spots during the autumn deer season.

Restrictions: Swimsuits are required in the two resort pools.

Access: The paved highway and access road make Belknap Hot Springs Resort accessible by any vehicle. Pool hours are 9:00 A.M. to 8:00 P.M.

Water temperature: Located across the McKenzie River from the swimming pools, the near-boiling hot springs flow at a temperature of 196° F. The two swimming pools are kept at 92° F. in summer and 102° F. in winter.

Services: The resort features several lodging options and mountain-bike rentals. The owners have been considering adding a restaurant to the main lodge, but currently you'll have to bring your own food (cooking facilities are provided in the

Belknap Hot Springs Resort

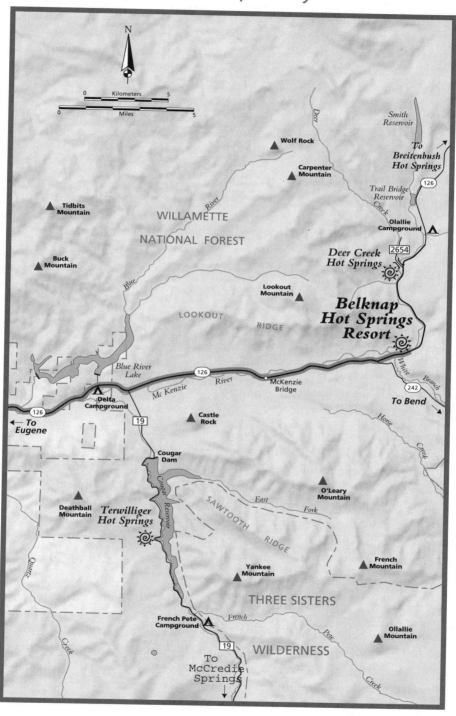

N

0   Kilometers   5
0   Miles   5

Smith
Reservoir

**To
Breitenbush
Hot Springs**

Deer

Wolf Rock

Carpenter
Mountain

126

Trail Bridge
Reservoir

Creek

Tidbits
Mountain

WILLAMETTE

Olallie
Campground

NATIONAL FOREST

2654

Deer Creek
Hot Springs

River

Buck
Mountain

Blue

Lookout
Mountain

*Belknap
Hot Springs
Resort*

LOOKOUT   RIDGE

Blue River
Lake

126

White

Branch

Mc Kenzie   River

McKenzie
Bridge

242

Delta
Campground

To Bend

126

**← To
Eugene**

19

Castle
Rock

Horse

Cougar
Dam

O'Leary
Mountain

Creek

Deathball
Mountain

*Terwilliger
Hot Springs*

Cougar

Reservoir

SAWTOOTH

East

Fork

RIDGE

French
Mountain

Quartz

Yankee
Mountain

THREE SISTERS

French Pete
Campground

French

Ollallie
Mountain

19

Pete

WILDERNESS

Creek

**To
McCredie
Springs**

Creek

cabins.) There are several restaurants within 5 miles of the resort for visitors who want to stay at the resort and let others take care of their meals.

Accommodations: The geothermally heated main lodge features twelve spacious rooms, most of which overlook the McKenzie River and the lower swimming pool. Three of the lodge rooms feature their own hot tubs supplied with mineral water from the hot springs. All rooms in the main lodge are nonsmoking.

Six cabins are available on the upper terrace behind the main lodge, near the upper warm-water swimming pool. The cabins vary in size and can sleep two to six. Several dozen camping sites and forty-nine full-service RV spots are also available on the upper terrace. Additional RV sites are located along the banks of the McKenzie River near the main lodge.

Map: Oregon State Highway Map.

Finding the springs: From Eugene drive 49 miles east on OR 126 to the town of McKenzie Bridge. Continue 6 miles east of the town of McKenzie Bridge, and turn left at the signs to Belknap resort. Drive 0.5 mile to the main lodge building on the shores of the McKenzie River.

Overview: Belknap Hot Springs has been a popular destination resort for Oregonians for more than 125 years. Since the 1870s the scalding hot springs on the north bank of the McKenzie have been piped across the river to a variety of bathhouses, soaking tubs, and the current two warm-water swimming pools. Day visitors can purchase an hourly or all-day pass to soak in the scenic lower pool.

East of the lower pool is a footbridge that leads across the McKenzie River to the source of the hot springs. Suspended from the bridge is the pipeline that brings the hot water from the springs to the resort. Past the hot springs are miles of hiking and biking trails that parallel the north side of the McKenzie River.

The upper terrace features several cabins and a second warm-water pool. It is also home to the Belknap Gardens, several acres of formal landscaping that features both native and cultivated plants. Plan on taking a stroll on the walkways through the gardens after a relaxing swim in the riverside pool.

History: Belknap Hot Springs were discovered in 1854 by explorers searching for the headwaters of the McKenzie River. The hot springs were originally called "Siloam Springs" or "The Pools of Salome." No commercial use of the hot springs occurred until Rollin Simeon Belknap claimed them in 1870. Originally from Vermont, Belknap moved to San Francisco during the famous gold rush of 1849. A few years later Belknap moved to southern Oregon, where he fought in the Rouge River Indian War in 1855. In 1870 Belknap claimed the hot springs as well as some level ground on the opposite bank of the McKenzie River. In 1872 Belknap moved his family to the property and built a hotel and bathhouse on the river's south bank. The hot springs on the opposite side of the river from the little resort were piped through a flume made of split cedar logs that Belknap suspended across the river.

Belknap promoted his new resort to residents in the nearby city of Eugene. The following advertisement appeared in the *Oregon State Journal* in 1874:

To Those in Search of
HEALTH OR PLEASURE
The undersigned, Proprietor of the

SILOAM SPRINGS

would call attention of those in search of health or pleasure to the properties and excellent situation of the above springs. They are situated on the McKenzie River, sixty miles east of Eugene City, surrounded by scenery beautiful and grand. The neighborhood abounds in game of every kind, and the streams with fine trout. The medicinal properties of the water have been tested by the cure of those who have visited them who have been afflicted with various disease, particularly Female Weakness, Scrofula, Rheumatism, Inflammations both external and internal, and general debility. Experienced males and females are always in attendance. Charges moderate. Good pasture near by.

R.S. Belknap, MD
John W. Sims. Proprietor

Belknap's marketing proved successful, and a horse-drawn stagecoach brought visitors from Eugene to the resort several times a week. The stagecoach ride took sixteen hours on bumpy dirt roads through the winding McKenzie River Valley.

Eventually Siloam Springs became better known as Belknap Hot Springs. Belknap sold the property only five years after building the hotel and bathhouse, but the resort still carries his name.

Belknap Hot Springs passed through several owners over the next three decades. The ownership stabilized in 1907, when a wealthy lumber baron from Michigan named John Hawk acquired the property. Three generations of Hawk's family managed the resort over the next sixty-eight years.

The 1950s and 1960s were the heyday of the resort's popularity. Betty Smith, proprietor of Belknap Springs during that time, recalled a typical summer: "Grandma and Pop came for the baths; Daddy fished and Mom knitted and the kids swam—it seemed like half of Eugene must have learned to swim up here."

Belknap Lodge and lower pool on the banks of the McKenzie River.

Smith operated the Belknap Hot Springs until 1967, when she closed the resort to the public. For the following eight years, the resort slumbered on the banks of the McKenzie River, with only a few of Smith's family members living on the property. In 1975 Smith sold Belknap Hot Springs to James Nation. Over the next three years, Nation rebuilt the neglected resort, reopening it to the public in 1978. Nation sold the property in 1995 to the McDougal family from Springfield, Oregon. The McDougals, who still own and manage Belknap Springs, have refurbished the swimming pools, lodge, and restaurant and have expanded the manicured flower gardens on the upper terrace.

Area attractions: Belknap's location near the center of the McKenzie River Valley provides a great base for a variety of recreational activities. The 30-mile-long McKenzie River Trail starts at Clear Lake and passes several scenic waterfalls as it parallels the McKenzie River. Guests at Belknap can bike or hike on this trail, which passes within a few yards of the resort. A bit farther from Belknap, in the Tamolich Valley, is a large sanctuary of old-growth Douglas fir trees. Whitewater rafting and fishing are within a few minutes' drive of the resort. Golfers can take advantage of the nearby Tokatee Golf Club, an 18-hole course.

Cross-country skiing is available nearby, and the Hoodoo Ski Bowl is located 25 miles east of Belknap on Santiam Pass.

Terwilliger (Cougar) Hot Springs

Contact information:
Blue River Ranger District
57600 Blue River Drive
P. O. Box 199
Blue River, OR 97413
(541) 822–3317
(Also visit the Friends of Cougar Hot Springs Web site: www.cougar.org.)

General description: A cascading series of hot soaking pools in a valley of old-growth cedars and Douglas fir.

Location: Oregon Cascades, 53 miles east of Eugene in the Willamette National Forest.

Development: The hot springs have been captured behind stair-stepped rock and log dams, but they still retain a rustic-wilderness feel. Two composting toilets are nearby, and a pegboard shelter adjacent to the pools provides a dry place to hang your clothes.

Best times to visit: You will often have the pools to yourself early in the morning, especially in the wintertime and on drizzly days. Avoid late afternoons, weekends, and holidays if you want to miss the crowds from nearby Eugene.

Restrictions: Terwilliger is perhaps the most tightly regulated of all public hot springs in the Pacific Northwest. From the 1960s through the mid-1990s, the hot springs were embroiled in a debate over management strategies. More than 14,000 people visited the springs annually. Semipermanent tent camps sprang up near the springs, with some visitors staying for weeks at a time. Violence and van-

Terwilliger (Cougar) Hot Springs

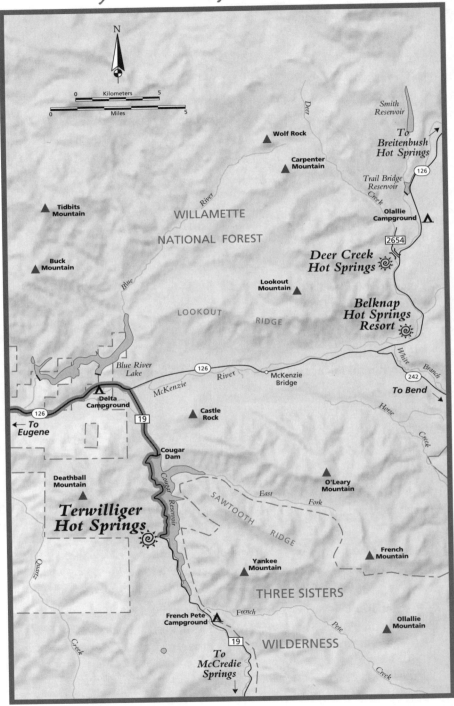

N

0 ____ Kilometers ____ 5

0 ____ Miles ____ 5

Wolf Rock

Carpenter Mountain

Deer

River

Smith Reservoir

To Breitenbush Hot Springs

126

Trail Bridge Reservoir

Creek

Tidbits Mountain

WILLAMETTE

NATIONAL FOREST

Olallie Campground

2654

Deer Creek Hot Springs

Buck Mountain

Blue

LOOKOUT

Lookout Mountain

RIDGE

Belknap Hot Springs Resort

White

Branch

Blue River Lake

126

McKenzie River

McKenzie Bridge

242

To Bend

Delta Campground

McKenzie

19

Castle Rock

Horse

Creek

126

To Eugene

Cougar Dam

Deathball Mountain

Cougar

Reservoir

SAWTOOTH

East

Fork

RIDGE

O'Leary Mountain

Terwilliger Hot Springs

French Mountain

Quartz

Yankee Mountain

THREE SISTERS

French Pete Campground

French

19

WILDERNESS

Ollallie Mountain

Pete

Creek

To McCredie Springs

Creek

dalism led the Forest Service to hold a series of public meetings in the 1990s to determine a better way to manage the hot springs.

In 1998 a day-use fee program was enacted, and camping was prohibited within 2 miles of the hot springs. Forest Service personnel began regular patrols of the area and leveled hefty fines on those who flouted the new rules.

Here's a summary of the current regulations at Terwilliger:

- A special Terwilliger Day Use Pass ($3.00 a day) must be purchased by all members of your party and carried on your person to the hot springs. A Northwest Forest Pass will substitute for the Terwilliger Day Use Pass, but only for the driver of the vehicle. All other passengers must purchase Terwilliger Day Use Passes. You can buy this pass at the hot springs parking area, at USFS ranger stations in Blue River and McKenzie Bridge, or at general stores and community markets in Blue River, Vida, Leaburg, and McKenzie Bridge. You must keep the passes in your possession while hiking to the hot springs. The Forest Service doesn't specify how to keep your pass with you if you're soaking in the nude, but don't be surprised if you're asked to pro-duce it. You may need to leave the steamy comfort of the soaking pools, scamper to the shelter where you hung your clothes, and pull the pass out of your pants pocket to prove that you've paid the fee.

- The Terwilliger area is for day use only, from sunrise to sunset. The USFS has posted a chart next to the hot springs showing the actual sunrise and sun-set times throughout the year. This chart helps the USFS avoid astrological arguments with bathers trying to squeeze in a few more minutes of soaking.

- No alcoholic beverages are allowed at the hot springs.

- No camping is allowed within 2 miles of the trailhead to the hot springs.

- Nudity is allowed only in the hot springs themselves. A USFS brochure warns that visible nudity is not allowed within sight of Aufderheide Scenic Byway. (Apparently there's a limit to what "scenery" can be tolerated on the Scenic Byway!)

Access: The hot springs are accessible year-round. Forest Service personnel drain and clean the soaking pools every Thursday in summer and every other Thursday in winter, so plan your visit for other days of the week. Occasional snows may block the access road for a few days in winter. It's an easy ten-minute hike on the gently sloping trail from the parking lot to the hot springs pools. Watch your step the last 10 yards when you cross the slippery rock dams that form the soaking pools.

Water temperature: The hot springs emerge from a small cave at about 116° F. The five successive soaking pools downhill from the cave usually vary from 106° in the top pool to 95° in the bottom pool. The pools can be up to five degrees warmer in summer months and several degrees cooler in rainy weather.

Services: No services are available at the hot springs except for composting toilets. Bring your own drinking water.

Accommodations: Camping accommodations only. Several seasonal campgrounds are located south of the hot springs parking area. Drive along the west side of Cougar Reservoir on FR 19 for 3.5 miles to reach the French Pete Campground. The more secluded Homestead Campground is 10 miles south of the hot springs on the banks of the South Fork of the McKenzie River. Several other USFS campgrounds are available even farther south on FR 19.

If you're looking for a spot for your tent closer to the McKenzie River Valley, USFS Delta Campground is located near the Cougar Reservoir turnoff from OR 126 (7.5 miles north of the hot springs parking area.)

Map: Willamette National Forest Map.

Finding the springs: From Eugene head east on OR 126 for 45 miles. Between Milepost 45 and 46 (about 4 miles past the town of Blue River), turn right onto Aufderheide Memorial Drive (FR 19). Drive 3.5 miles south on FR 19 until you reach Cougar Dam. Turn right at the dam and stay on FR 19. Drive 4.3 miles from the dam along the west side of Cougar Reservoir to the Terwilliger parking area. Park your car and purchase Terwilliger Day Passes at the information booth if you don't already have them (bring $3.00 cash per person). Although there is significantly less vandalism in the parking area now than in past years, it's still wise to place all valuables in your car trunk or take them with you to the hot springs. Grab your towels and walk north along the side of FR 19 for about a hundred yards to the trailhead for the hot springs (the Cougar Reservoir will be on the right, and the lagoon and waterfall formed by Rider Creek will be on the left). The hike from the trailhead to the hot springs is less than half a mile through a beautiful grove of cedars and Douglas fir.

A public-transit bus from Eugene stops at the Cougar Reservoir turnoff on OR 126 about 7.5 miles from the hot springs. On weekends college kids from the University of Oregon often ride this bus in the morning to the turnoff, then hitchhike or bike to the hot springs (the transit bus has bike racks). The transit bus picks up riders in the evening for the trip back to Eugene. Call (541) 687–5555 to obtain the daily bus schedule.

Overview: The popularity of Terwilliger Hot Springs is well deserved. The hushed stillness of the old-growth forest surrounding the hiking trail prepares visitors for the steamy soaks that await. The trail emerges near the uppermost hot pool, which, like all the pools, can hold five to ten people. The upper pool collects the hot springs water that flows from a small grotto (adventurous visitors sometimes crawl into this grotto, although the 113° F. water there usually drives them out in a few minutes). Overflow from the upper pool forms a waterfall that drops 5 feet into the next pool. Three other pools follow in succession, each enclosed by a rock-and-log dam that keeps the pools between 1 and 3 feet deep. There's very little sulphur odor to the hot springs. The soaking pools rest on solid granite slabs, and there's little mud or debris to cloud the crystalline hot water. It's easy to find your preferred soaking temperature, because each pool is about 5° F. cooler than the pool above it. The Friends of Cougar Hot Springs and the USFS have built rustic log-and-stone steps to aid navigation between the hot pools.

If you've visiting Terwilliger on a hot summer day in July or August, consider taking a dip in the nearby freshwater lagoon to cool off from the steamy waters of the springs. The lagoon is located at the base of the waterfall formed by Rider Creek. You can access the lagoon on several side trails leading off the main trail to the hot springs. All motorcraft are banned in the lagoon, so you can swim without worrying about jet skis or fishing boats passing nearby.

History: Terwilliger Hot Springs have been known by a variety of names. Capra Hot Springs appears to be one of the earliest monikers, followed by Rider Creek Hot Springs, South Fork Hot Springs, and most recently Cougar Hot Springs (so named because of the hot springs' proximity to Cougar Reservoir). Cougar Hot Springs is the name still used by many visitors, and a volunteer group called "Friends of Cougar Hot Springs" was formed in 1998 to help protect and maintain the soaking pools and hiking trail.

The USFS officially calls the area Terwilliger Hot Springs, named for Hiram Terwilliger who came to Oregon in the 1860s and is thought to have been the first European to visit the hot springs. In 1906 Terwilliger filed a mineral-rights claim to the hot springs, but the Forest Service denied the claim, stating that Terwilliger's true intention was to build a summer resort on the property (a use not allowed under the mining law). Apparently the Forest Service changed its regulation two decades later, when in 1927 a special-use permit to construct a resort was issued to A. J. Jacobs of Eugene. Even with permit in hand, Jacobs never developed the property commercially, and the pristine hot springs remained little known.

For decades, visiting Terwilliger Hot Springs was a difficult proposition. Only the most committed travelers attempted the narrow trail along the South Fork of the McKenzie River. The isolated nature of Terwilliger Hot Springs abruptly changed in the 1960s, when the U.S. Army Corps of Engineers constructed a dam on the South Fork of the McKenzie to form Cougar Reservoir. A paved road was built from OR 126 along the west side of the new reservoir, which passed within a half mile of Terwilliger Hot Springs. Once the new road was finished, visitor use to Terwilliger skyrocketed.

From the 1960s through the 1990s, the hot springs increased in popularity. Visitors set up semipermanent tent villages near the springs. As many as 1,000 people were rumored to live in tents within a quarter mile of the hot springs. In

Soaking pools at Terwilliger Hot Springs.

1997 members of the counterculture Rainbow Family scheduled their annual gathering near the springs, which attracted thousands of revelers. Although most visitors during these years were peaceful, a few individuals caused problems. The USFS received an increasing number of reports of trash, illicit drug use, sexual assault, vandalism, panhandling, and noisy parties. The rowdy incidents peaked in 1996, when a man was killed by a neighboring camper who was angry at the late-night partying and loud music.

The increase in crowds and violence led the USFS to hold several public meetings to carve out a new management policy. In 1998 fees and restrictions on camping were imposed on the hot springs area, which quickly brought an end to the semipermanent tent communities that had surrounded the hot springs. The fee system also provided funds that allowed the Forest Service to clean up the trash left by large crowds over the years, as well as rebuild the soaking pools. At present most visitors feel that Terwilliger Hot Springs is much cleaner and safer than it has been in the past forty years.

Area attractions: Aufderheide Memorial Drive (FR 19) is one of the most scenic roads in the Oregon Cascades. The Blue River Ranger District office will lend you a free audiocassette that gives you a mile-by-mile description of the natural wonders along this roadway. The 58-mile drive passes by Terwilliger Hot Springs, then climbs for 15 miles through old-growth Douglas fir to summit near Box

Canyon Guard Station. Most day-trippers from Eugene turn around at the summit, but if you have extra time (and good brakes), continue on the winding descent for 32 miles to the towns of Oakridge and Westfir. McCredie and Wall Creek hot springs are only a few minutes' drive from Oakridge, so consider combining these popular soaks with your visit to Terwilliger to make a nice weekend getaway.

Wall Creek Hot Springs (Meditation Pool)

Contact Information:
Middle Fork Ranger District
46375 Highway 58
Westfir, OR 97492
(541) 782–2283

General description: A peaceful creekside soaking pool surrounded by old-growth forest.

Location: Oregon Cascades, 51 miles southeast of Eugene.

Development: The pool around the natural warm springs has been enlarged to accommodate several bathers, and volunteers have built a crude rock dam to raise the soaking level. These small improvements don't detract from the primeval experience of soaking in an isolated glen of old-growth forest.

Best times to visit: Warm days in spring, summer, and autumn. Tepid water temperatures make this an uncomfortably chilly soak in winter.

Restrictions: A Northwest Forest Pass is required to visit Wall Creek Hot Springs. (Purchase the pass at the ranger stations in Oakridge or Lowell prior to driving to the trailhead.) The trail and hot springs are day-use areas only.

Access: Any vehicle can make the easy drive on highway and blacktop roads to the parking area at the trailhead. The hike is a gentle twenty-minute walk.

Water temperature: The warm-springs pool varies from 94° to 98° F.

Services: None available at the springs. Food and gas can be purchased in Oakridge, 10 miles south of the trailhead.

Wall Creek Hot Springs

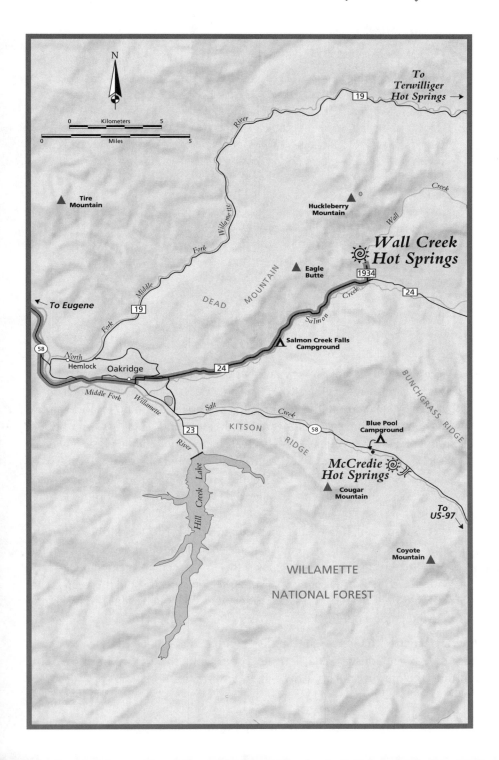

N

Kilometers
0   5

Miles
0   5

To
Terwilliger
Hot Springs →

19

Tire
Mountain

River

Willamette

Fork

Middle

Fork

Creek

Huckleberry
Mountain

Wall

Wall Creek
Hot Springs

1934

24

DEAD   MOUNTAIN

Eagle
Butte

Creek

Salmon

To Eugene

19

58

North
Hemlock

Oakridge

24

Salmon Creek Falls
Campground

BUNCHGRASS RIDGE

Middle Fork   Willamette

Salt

Creek

KITSON   RIDGE

58

Blue Pool
Campground

23

River

Hill Creek Lake

McCredie
Hot Springs

To
US-97 →

Cougar
Mountain

Coyote
Mountain

WILLAMETTE

NATIONAL FOREST

Accommodations: No camping is allowed along the trail or next to the hot springs. Salmon Creek Falls Campground, which is open from late April to mid-October, is located 5 miles south of the hot springs trailhead on FR 24. Motels are available in nearby Oakridge.

Map: Willamette National Forest map.

Finding the springs: From Eugene drive 40 miles east on OR 58 to Oakridge. Turn left off the highway at Oakridge's only stoplight, drive over the railroad track overpass, and turn right onto East First Street. Drive east on East First Street through the main business district of Oakridge. From the east boundary of Oakridge, East First Street turns into FR 24 (it's a nicely paved two-lane road). Drive on FR 24 for 9.1 miles on the winding two-lane road parallel to Salmon Creek. When you cross the bridge over Wall Creek, turn left on FR 1934 at the Blair Lake turnoff. Drive 0.5 miles on FR 1934 (it's a dirt road). Turn left into the small parking area marked by a hiking-trail sign. Place your Northwest Forest Pass on the dashboard and lock your valuables in your trunk.

The hiking trail from the parking area to the warm springs is a gentle 600-yard stroll. Douglas fir, hemlocks, maples, and moss-covered cedars line the trail. The hiking trail follows Wall Creek, ending in a small clearing that contains the warm springs pool.

Overview: Wall Creek Hot Springs slumber on the banks of a fast-flowing stream. The soaking pool is about 10 feet wide and 3 feet deep, with perhaps half a dozen bubbling hot-water vents in the center of the pool. There's no noticeable sulphur odor to the water. The water temperature hovers around 95° F.—warm, but not hot enough for a good winter soak. The oval-shaped pool is about 12 feet wide by 15 feet long. A sheet of black plastic at the end of the pool closest to Wall Creek helps dam the warm-water overflow, keeping the pool level up to about 3 feet. Large river rocks encircle the pool's edge. The pool can easily accommodate five or six bathers.

There's also a small hot-water seep (about 102° F.) 10 feet farther down the banks of Wall Creek from the main soaking pool. The lethargic flow rate of this seep (and the scum-covered rocks) makes this lower seep an unappetizing soak.

With the gentle sounds of nearby Wall Creek rushing by and the deep-green, moss-covered trees overhead, it's easy to see why Wall Creek Hot Springs is also called "Meditation Pool."

Area attractions: McCredie Hot Springs is situated about 10 miles east of Oakridge off OR 58. Consider a day-long hot springs tour, soaking at McCredie in the morning (before the crowds arrive), then visiting the lesser-known Wall Creek

Wall Creek Hot Springs (also called Meditation Pool).

Hot Springs in the afternoon. Waldo Lake Wilderness and Diamond Peak Wilderness are about 20 miles east of Oakridge. Waldo Lake, Odell Lake, and Crescent Lake attract fishermen and boaters.

McCredie Hot Springs

Contact information:
Middle Fork Ranger District
46375 Highway 58
Westfir, OR 97492
(541) 782–2283

General description: Accessible hot soaking pools that flank both sides of a picturesque mountain stream.

Location: Oregon Cascades, 51 miles southeast of Eugene.

Development: McCredie Hot Springs was a popular commercial resort until the 1960s, but all signs of the hotel and swimming pool are long gone. Volunteers have dug primitive soaking pools to capture outflow from the numerous hot springs along the banks of Salt Creek.

Best times to visit: Soaking at McCredie is popular year-round. Avoid holidays and weekends if you're seeking solitude. The secluded soaking pools on the south side of Salt Creek are less visited than pools near the highway.

Restrictions: The McCredie parking area and hot springs are located on USFS land and are closed from sunset to sunrise. Overnight camping is not permitted at the springs or in the adjacent parking area. A Northwest Forest Pass is not required.

Access: Any vehicle can make the trip on OR 58 to the parking area. It's a five-minute stroll from your car to the hot springs. Truck drivers often stop for a soak, as it's one of the few hot springs with a parking area large enough to handle the big 18-wheelers.

Water temperature: The hot springs at McCredie vary in temperature from 100° F. to 160° F. Most of the soaking pools average a comfortable 100° to 105° F.

McCredie Hot Springs

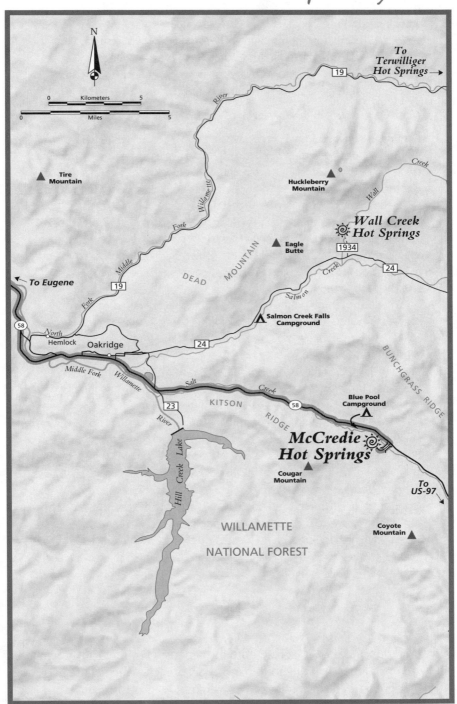

N

Kilometers 0 — 5

Miles 0 — 5

To Terwilliger Hot Springs →

19

Tire Mountain

Huckleberry Mountain

River

Willamette

Fork

Middle

DEAD MOUNTAIN

Eagle Butte

Wall Creek

Wall Creek Hot Springs

1934

24

Salmon Creek Falls Campground

Salmon Creek

To Eugene

19

North Fork

58

Hemlock

Oakridge

24

Middle Fork Willamette

Salt Creek

KITSON RIDGE

58

Blue Pool Campground

BUNCHGRASS RIDGE

23

River

Hill Creek Lake

McCredie Hot Springs

Cougar Mountain

To US-97 →

WILLAMETTE

NATIONAL FOREST

Coyote Mountain

Services: No services are available at the hot springs. Restaurants, supplies, and gas can be found in Oakridge, 9.5 miles west of the hot springs on OR 58.

Accommodations: The Blue Pool Campground, maintained by the USFS, is located 0.5 mile west of the hot springs. The campground is open from mid-May to October. You can easily walk to the hot springs from the campground, so consider staying there a night or two and spend your daylight hours soaking at McCredie. Motels are available in nearby Oakridge.

Map: Oregon State Highway Map.

Finding the springs: From Eugene drive south on I–5 for 3 miles to the Oakridge exit (OR 58, also called the Willamette Highway.) Drive southeast for 40 miles to the town of Oakridge. From the stoplight in Oakridge, continue driving southeast on OR 58 for another 9.4 miles to the USFS Blue Pool Campground. Continue another 0.5 mile on OR 58 past the campground to Milepost 45. Look for a large parking lot just past Milepost 45 on the south side of the road, near a sign marked MCCREDIE STATION ROAD. Pull into the parking lot. The trail to the hot springs is located at the east side of the parking lot. Lock your car, grab your towel, and walk about 50 yards along a dirt path that parallels Salt Creek to the soaking pools.

If the soaking pools on the north side of Salt Creek are filled with fellow hot springs enthusiasts, then give the hot springs on the other side of Salt Creek a try. To reach these hot springs, walk back to the main parking lot, then drive 0.5 miles southeast on OR 58. Turn south onto Shady Gap Road, and cross the bridge spanning Salt Creek. Turn west (right) just after crossing the bridge onto FR 5875. Drive for 0.1 mile toward the first sharp left curve in the road. There's a DAY USE ONLY sign barely visible in the trees to the right (toward Salt Creek). Park your car on the wide pullout just past the sign, then walk back a few yards from your car until you see a faint trail heading down the bank and downstream along Salt Creek. Follow this trail for about 500 yards (keep left at the two branches in the trail) until you reach the shaded soaking pools on the south bank of Salt Creek. You'll see the more heavily visited soaking pools across the creek about 100 yards to the north. (*Caution:* It's tempting to wade across Salt Creek from the north-bank soaking pools to the more secluded pools on the south bank, but the fast-moving current in the creek can be treacherous. Be safe and take an extra fifteen minutes to drive across the bridge and hike the trail to reach the soaking pools on the south side of the creek.)

Overview: The 50-yard walking path from the parking lot by the highway will bring you to an open terrace on the north bank of Salt Creek, which contains a variety of soaking opportunities. Hemlocks, cedars, and Douglas fir separate the sunny,

The large soaking pool on the north bank of Salt Creek at McCredie Hot Springs.

open stream bank from the highway, which lies 100 yards north of the soaking area. A car or truck may occasionally be seen through the trees on the highway, but for the most part the traffic has little impact on the soaking experience.

The largest of McCredie's soaking pools is a crowd pleaser that's about 20 feet wide by 40 feet long. Three separate hot springs on the edge of this pool keep the soaking temperature around a comfortable 105° F, and several smaller vents bubble in the pool itself. Some of the hot springs that supply the soaking pools at McCredie exceed a scalding 160° F., so test the pools before you get in and avoid getting too close to the hot springs vents. The pool averages 100° to 105° F., depending on how close you sit to a hot springs vent. There's a slight sulphur smell in all of the pools at McCredie, but it's quite tame compared with the smell in some other hot springs in the Cascades. The large soaking pool varies in depth from 1 to 2 feet.

About 20 yards upstream from the main pool is a second sizable soaking opportunity—a 20-foot-diameter circular pool that can hold a modest (or immodest) crowd. This pool is slightly less popular than the large soaking pool.

Bordering Salt Creek are two or three rock pools suitable for one to two people. These small pools capture hot water from 150° F. springs that flow into the creek. Cold water from the creek mixes with the hot springs water in these pools, resulting in a comfortable 100° F. average temperature.

The more secluded hot springs on the south side of Salt Creek are also well worth checking out, especially if the north-side pools get too busy. The main

Children playing in an outdoor log tub at McCredie Hot Springs in 1931.
PHOTO: COURTESY OREGON HISTORICAL SOCIETY

source of geothermal heat on the south bank is a 125° F. spring issuing from the base of a low, lichen-covered support wall of river rock and concrete. This crumbling foundation wall is all that is left of the old McCredie Springs Lodge and swimming pool. The main spring flows into a pool about 10 feet in diameter and 1 foot deep. Temperature in this pool is a comfortable 100° to 105° F. A rock dam separates this main pool from a slightly smaller (and slightly cooler) lower pool. These two pools lie in a shady grove of cedars, maples, and Douglas fir. It's certainly more secluded and peaceful in these pools than in those on the sunny north side of Salt Creek.

History: In 1878 a trapper named Frank Warner discovered the hot springs while following a Native American trail along Salt Creek. Warner built a cabin near the springs but apparently did no other development to the property. When the national forest system was established in the early 1900s, the hot springs were declared public property.

John Hardin, a builder from Eugene, filed a placer claim on the hot springs in 1911. (Under existing mining law anyone who found salt deposits on public land could file a mining claim.) Hardin was given a mining lease on the property, but his real intention was to build a resort near the hot springs. By 1914 Hardin had completed construction of a two-story hotel that could house sixty guests. The hotel featured a large porch that reached along the entire south side of the hotel and overlooked Salt Creek. Large doors opened up onto the porch from each bedroom so that a bed could be rolled out on the porch on hot summer days to take advantage of any cool breezes near the creek.

In 1916 the lease for the resort was transferred to Judge Walter McCredie, a colorful character from Portland who owned a semipro baseball team. The judge would often would bring his team members to the resort to enjoy the benefits of the hot water. Although McCredie managed the resort for only five years, the hot springs are still associated with his name.

The Southern Pacific Railway, built through the valley in 1923, passed within a few yards of McCredie Hot Springs. This opened up the entire area to tourists from Eugene and Portland. During the heyday of the McCredie Hot Springs resort in the late 1930s, five trains stopped daily near the resort.

The McCredie resort continued to operate through the 1940s and 1950s, although it suffered through a series of poor managers. The resort developed a particularly unsavory reputation in the late 1940s, when a woman described by a Forest Service representative as "one of the most impossible persons we have ever known" managed the property. According to a cultural history produced by the Forest Service, the woman ran a bordello out of the resort, with three daily shifts of prostitutes—"one working, one coming, and one going." Although the resort's manager was repeatedly jailed for running a house of prostitution, she always managed to make bail and was "as slippery as an eel at evading the law." The deputy sheriff in nearby Oakridge stated that the woman had alone "caused his office more trouble than the entire population of Oakridge and Westfir, with fringe areas put together, some eight to ten thousand people."

Even though the Forest Service officials were aware of the shenanigans at McCredie, they failed to shut down the bordello. The cultural history written by the Forest Service noted that "she had guns and boasted she knew how to use them. Forest Service officials seemed to prefer to remain healthy."

The feisty manager of the resort left peacefully in the 1950s, when George Owen acquired the lease. Owen's tenure at McCredie was filled with tragedy. Fire destroyed the hotel in 1958, and a flood on Christmas Day in 1964 washed out the bridge across Salt Creek and destroyed the swimming pool. The Forest Service terminated Owen's lease shortly after the flood and then burned or removed all remaining buildings on the property. At present only the concrete foundations of the old hotel are visible near the soaking pools on the south side of Salt Creek.

Area Attractions: Wall Creek Hot Springs is located about ten miles north of Oakridge. A weekend trip could include visiting both Wall Creek Hot Springs and McCredie Hot Springs and staying in one of the many area campgrounds or at one of the motels in Oakridge. Great hiking opportunities are available in nearby Waldo Lake Wilderness and Diamond Peak Wilderness, about a half-hour east of Oakridge. Fishing and boating are popular activities at Waldo Lake, Odell Lake, and Crescent Lake.

14

Umpqua Hot Springs

Contact information:
Diamond Lake Ranger District
2020 Toketee Ranger Station Road
Idleyld Park, OR 97447
(541) 498–2531

General description: A forest soaking pool atop a 100-foot terrace that overlooks North Umpqua River.

Location: Oregon Cascades, 60 miles east of Roseburg, 30 miles west of Crater Lake National Park.

Development: The hot springs are undeveloped, except for the primitive three-sided shelter that encloses the main soaking pool.

Best times to visit: The Forest Service conducted a user survey of Umpqua Hot Springs in 1998 and found that close to 9,000 people visited the springs that year. This represented an increase in visitors of 45 percent in three years. Try to visit in the early mornings and in the middle of the week to avoid crowds. You may have to wait your turn to soak in the hot springs on holidays and weekends. Cooler days in autumn, winter, and spring may be more enjoyable for soaking in the 106° to 115° F. pools. (There is no cold-water source to reduce the pool temperature, so a soak on a hot summer day may not be as enjoyable as it would be during cooler weather.)

Restrictions: A Northwest Forest Pass is required for all vehicles parked at the Umpqua Hot Springs parking area ($5.00 for a day pass, $30.00 for an annual pass). No camping is allowed at the hot springs. No motorized vehicles are allowed on the access trail. Nudity is common in the soaking pools.

Access: The hot springs are open year-round, twenty-four hours a day. Any vehicle can make the trip on the paved and gravel roads to the Umpqua Hot Springs

Umpqua Hot Springs

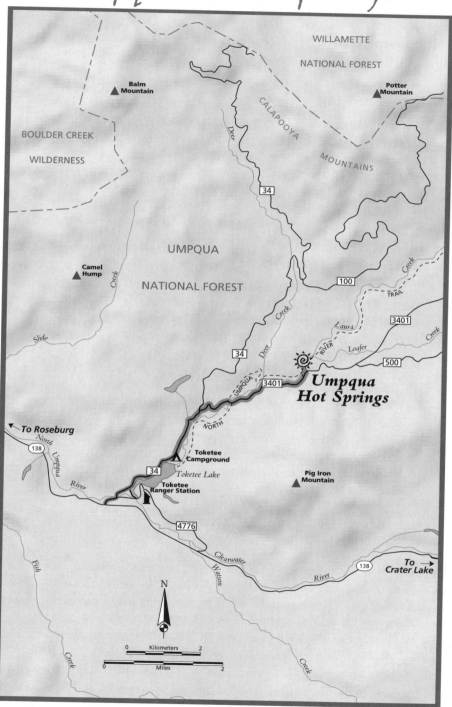

WILLAMETTE

NATIONAL FOREST

Balm
Mountain

Potter
Mountain

BOULDER CREEK

WILDERNESS

CALAPOOYA

MOUNTAINS

Deer

34

UMPQUA

Camel
Hump

NATIONAL FOREST

Creek

Creek

Deer Creek

100

TRAIL

3401

Laura

34

UMPQUA

Deer

RIVER

Loafer

Creek

Slide

3401

500

**Umpqua
Hot Springs**

NORTH

To Roseburg

North

138

Toketee
Campground

Umpqua

River

34

Toketee Lake

Pig Iron
Mountain

Toketee
Ranger Station

4776

N

Fish

Watson

Clearwater

River

138

Creek

To
Crater Lake

Creek

0   Kilometers   2

0   Miles   2

parking area, although occasional winter snows can block the last few miles of road. The 0.3-mile hiking trail is a bit steep the last 200 yards before reaching the hot springs.

Water temperature: The temperature in the soaking pools varies between 100° and 115° F., with temperatures between 106° and 110° F. most common.

Services: There's a composting toilet located a few yards from the hot springs, but there are no other services in the area.

Accommodations: Camping accommodations only. A few unofficial camping spots are located across the North Umpqua River downstream from the hot springs. (You may be able to see some tents from the Umpqua Hot Springs soaking pools.) To reach these riverside camping spots, take the trail that forks downhill from near the composting toilet adjacent to the hot springs.

There's another camping area at Toketee Campground, 2.5 miles southwest of the hot springs parking area at the head of the Toketee Reservoir. A fee is charged to camp at Toketee Campground.

Maps: Oregon State Highway Map, Umpqua National Forest Recreation Map.

Finding the springs: From Roseburg head east on OR 138 for 60 miles. Turn north on FR 34 for 1.4 miles to the Tokatee Ranger Station. (Stop at the Ranger Station to pick up campground information and to purchase a Forest Pass, if you don't already have one.) Continue north past the Ranger Station on FR 34 for 2.2 miles, passing over two concrete bridges that span the Clearwater River. Turn northwest onto FR 3401, which follows the north side of Toketee Reservoir, and drive 2 miles until you see the Umpqua Hot Springs parking area on the left side of the road. Park your car and put your Northwest Forest Service Pass on the dashboard. Take the hiking trail north of the parking area across the footbridge spanning the North Umpqua River, and hike 0.1 mile to a trail junction. You're now on the North Umpqua River Trail, a popular hike that parallels the river for 80 miles. Turn right at the junction and hike next to the river, heading upstream for 0.2 mile to the hot springs. The last few hundred yards of the trail are fairly steep.

Overview: Few hot springs in the Pacific Northwest are as scenic as Umpqua. Over thousands of years the mineral water on the banks of the North Umpqua River has deposited a travertine mound more than 100 feet tall. The hot springs emerge from the top of this terrace and flow into four soaking pools.

The main pool, enclosed by a three-sided log shelter, is approximately 5 feet wide by 8 feet long and 2 to 3 feet deep. It can easily hold four or five people. This is the most popular pool, both because of the comfortable soaking temperature and the view of the river valley. The hot springs source is located in a fissure in

Umpqua Hot Springs, overlooking the North Umpqua River.

the travertine about 10 yards above the main pool. The hot water is piped from the rock fissure to the pool through a rubber hose. If you're squeamish about bathing in the shallow soaking pool in hot water that has been used by other bathers, you can use one of the ten-gallon buckets next to the shelter to bail out the water, then let the pool refill with fresh hot water from the hose.

Above the sheltered pool is a smaller (and hotter) pool that holds two to three people. This pool is often empty because the water sometimes approaches 115° F., a bit too toasty for most visitors. An even smaller pool takes the overflow from the small pool, and it is somewhat cooler. There's a fourth pool clinging to the side of the terrace about 20 yards downhill toward the river that collects the runoff from the other three pools. Be careful when walking around the pools on the terrace, especially during rainy weather when the travertine is quite slick. It's a long fall to the river valley below.

History: According to a local county history, a settler named Perry Wright homesteaded near the hot springs. Wright's wife, Jessie, recalled that Native Americans used to bathe in the natural basin of hot water. The Wrights would also bathe in the springs in summer, when they were pasturing their cattle in a nearby meadow.

In the early 1900s a Forest Service employee named Carlos Neal was stationed at a fire lookout near the hot springs. Neal would often soak in the shallow natural soaking pool but was dissatisfied with its depth. He decided to enlarge the pool and packed a hammer and chisel with him during his visits to travertine terrace. Neal chiseled a 3-foot-deep soaking basin into the soft rock during the several summers that he was stationed in the area. The Forest Service later built a three-sided log shelter over the hot springs. Over the years the bark has worn away from the logs that make up the walls of the shelter, replaced with hundreds of initials carved into the wood by visitors to the hot springs.

It's doubtful that Forest Service employees today would be allowed to "improve" natural hot springs in the same way that Neal did in the early 1900s. Fortunately the mineral-water deposits in the subsequent decades have softened the rough chisel marks on the edges of the pool, and bathers usually don't realize that the soaking basin is anything but natural.

In the 1990s three other smaller soaking pools were built, two of them located behind the sheltered pool. A third pool has been built in the runoff channel about 30 yards down the steep slope of the travertine terrace

Area attractions: The Umpqua National Forest is home to an amazing variety of outdoor recreational opportunities. Crater Lake National Park lies less than an hour from Umpqua Hot Springs. The North Umpqua River Trail features many access points along OR 138, making it perfect for day hikes or a weeklong trek. The North Umpqua River is popular with rafters and with fisherman pursuing steelhead salmon. Winter turns many area hiking trails into snow-covered paths popular with cross-country skiers, and a half-dozen "snoparks" between Toketee Lake and Crater Lake National Park give snowmobilers a variety of backcountry recreation opportunities.

WellSprings
(Jackson Hot Springs)

Contact information:
WellSprings
2253 Highway 99 North
Ashland, Oregon 97520
(808) 482–3776
wellspringsnet.com

General description: A historic mineral-water swimming pool and campground that is slowly being rebuilt into an integrated health retreat.

Location: Southwest Oregon, 2 miles north of Ashland.

Development: The hot springs have been used commercially since the late 1800s.

Best times to visit: The WellSprings campground and swimming pool are open year-round. The Springs Café is closed in winter.

Restrictions: A fee is charged to use the swimming pool. Swimsuits are required in the pool. The private hot tubs are clothing-optional.

Access: WellSprings is adjacent to OR 99, so any vehicle can make the trip.

Water temperature: The 100° F. hot springs bubble to the surface in a fenced pool behind the resort. The swimming-pool temperature is kept around 80° F. The hot springs water temperature is boosted up to 120° F. for use in the private hot tubs (the tubs can be individually adjusted with cold water to a comfortable soaking temperature).

Services: A large greenhouse and nearby gardens provide organic produce for the Springs Café. The campground features rest rooms, showers, and laundry facilities. Gas, groceries, and restaurants are available in nearby Ashland.

WellSprings (Jackson Hot Springs)

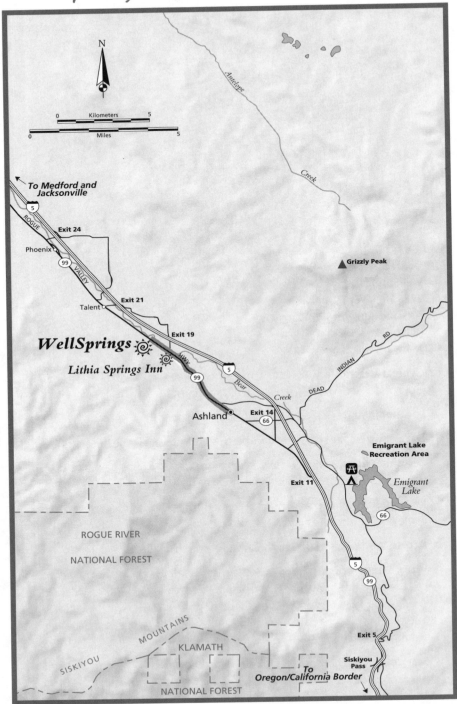

N

Kilometers
0   5
Miles
0   5

Antelope

Creek

**To Medford and
Jacksonville**

5

ROGUE

Exit 24

Phoenix

99

VALLEY

▲ **Grizzly Peak**

Exit 21

Talent

Exit 19

WellSprings ☀

Hwy

Lithia Springs Inn ☀

99

5

Bear

Creek

INDIAN

RD

DEAD

Ashland

Exit 14
66

**Emigrant Lake
Recreation Area**

*Emigrant
Lake*

Exit 11

66

ROGUE RIVER

NATIONAL FOREST

5

99

MOUNTAINS

KLAMATH

Exit 5

SISKIYOU

**Siskiyou
Pass**

*To
Oregon/California Border*

NATIONAL FOREST

Accommodations: WellSprings has twenty RV sites with full hookups and thirty tent camping spots shaded by pine, oak, and laurel trees. Eleven small cabins next to the RV sites at one time housed guests but were damaged in a 1997 New Year's Day flood. The current owners hope to renovate six of the cabins to make them once again available to resort visitors.

Map: Oregon State Highway Map.

Finding the springs: From downtown Ashland drive 2 miles north on OR 99 to a stoplight and junction with I–5. Continue north on OR 99 another 200 yards. Look for a large yellow sign marking the turn to Jackson Hot Springs on the left side of the road. Turn into the lane and drive about 50 yards down the lane to the WellSprings pool building.

Overview: WellSprings is still known to most locals by its old name of Jackson Hot Springs. The name was officially changed in 1995 by its two new owners: Gerry Lehrburger, a physician who specializes in "integrative medicines"; and Bruce Blackwell, an acupuncturist and Chinese herbalist. Lehrburger and Blackwell have been slowly transforming the resort into a nonprofit health and research center. They have plans to build an outdoor soaking pool, offer dance therapies, and conduct classes in tai chi, aikido, and yoga. The thirty-acre property seems to be in a constant state of construction, and the needed money to make major renovations to the old buildings has been difficult to raise. The new owners, however, are confident that WellSprings will one day be a nationally known health retreat.

The biggest attraction at WellSprings is the warm-water swimming pool. The 50-foot by 100-foot open-air pool, built in the 1920s, is maintained at 80° F. year-round.

Adjacent to the pool are two indoor private soaking tubs available for hourly rental. An organic food cafe is open during summer, supplied with fresh produce from a 3,000-square-foot greenhouse and organic garden located behind the cafe.

History: Jackson is one of the few hot springs resorts remaining from the heyday of Ashland's mineral-springs era. In 1886 a visitor to Ashland described the importance of mineral water to the area:

The region is particularly rich in soda and sulphur springs, both cold and thermal, and is fast becoming a resort for invalids, tourists, and those in search of the healing waters of nature. The opening of through railroad communications will, in the near future, bring thousands from abroad to the fountains of life.

The main entrance to the WellSprings swimming pool.

Several hot springs and mineral springs resorts developed in and around Ashland, including Wagner's Soda Springs, Buckhorn Springs, Helman Baths, White Sulphur Springs, Dead Indian Springs, and Kingsbury Springs.

John Barrett claimed Jackson Hot Springs and the surrounding land in 1857. Thirty years later Barrett sold the land to G. F. Billings. Billings's granddaughter, Eugenia Jackson, eventually inherited the hot springs and surrounding ranchland. She sold the springs to Jacob and Gertrude Ottinger, on the condition that the name "Jackson Hot Springs" remain with the property. The Ottingers built a public swimming pool, an outdoor dance pavilion, and small rental cabins. Unfortunately all these buildings burned to the ground in 1933.

The Ottingers rebuilt the pool building and cabins and continued to manage the hot springs until 1960, when the property was sold to William Wallace and Ruth Smith, who managed the facility into the 1980s. In 1995 the resort was sold to the Jackson WellSprings, the current owners.

Area attractions: Ashland offers a wide variety of cultural activities that include the Oregon Shakespeare Festival, which runs from February through October, several music festivals, and a host of art galleries and museums. Less than 10 miles north of WellSprings lies the gold-rush town of Jacksonville, which has more than eighty buildings on the National Register of Historic Places. Jacksonville is home to the Britt Festival, a summer-long outdoor music and performing-arts gathering that features nationally known artists.

Lithia Springs Inn

Contact information:
Lithia Springs Inn
2165 West Jackson Road
Ashland, OR 97520
(800) 482–7128 or (541) 482–7128
www.lithiaspringsinn.com

General description: A charming country inn with naturally heated mineral-water whirlpool tubs in the guest cottages. The inn is a great getaway for a romantic weekend, which could include attending the Oregon Shakespeare Festival in nearby Ashland.

Location: Southwest Oregon, 2 miles north of Ashland.

Development: Individual cottages and well-manicured grounds surround a main lodge.

Best times to visit: The Inn is open year-round. During Ashland's popular Oregon Shakespeare Festival (February to November), room reservations should be made as far ahead of time as possible.

Restrictions: The spring-fed soaking tubs in the cottages are reserved for over-night guests of the inn.

Access: The resort is a few hundred yards from OR 99. Any vehicle can make the trip.

Water temperature: The well behind the inn provides 96° F. water to the resort. The water temperature is boosted another 20° F. prior to being piped to the soaking tubs in the guest cottages.

Services: A full breakfast is included with the lodging, and home-baked pastries and other snacks are available throughout the day. Fuel and many excellent restaurants are available in nearby Ashland.

Lithia Springs Inn

Accommodations: Lithia Springs Inn has fourteen well-appointed rooms. Most of the rooms have double whirlpool tubs, and some have a fireplace. The most elegant lodging option is the Emperor's Room, which features rare oriental antiques, a black faux-marble fireplace, and an entire wall covered with a hand-carved scene of the Imperial Palace of China.

Map: Oregon State Highway Map.

Finding the springs: From downtown Ashland drive 2 miles north on OR 99 toward Medford. A few yards past the stoplight across from Town and Country Chevrolet, turn left onto the unmarked West Jackson Road and follow the white-board fence down this gravel lane for 200 yards to the parking lot of Lithia Springs Inn.

Overview: Whereas nearby WellSprings caters to the counterculture and RV crowd, the Lithia Springs Inn targets a better-heeled clientele. Proprietor Duane Smith was at one time a real-estate developer and part owner of neighboring Jackson Hot Springs. In 1991 Smith sold his stake ownership in Jackson Hot Springs and purchased land to the south, where he drilled a well and discovered a nice flow of 100° F. water. After building the Lithia Springs Inn, Smith began advertising the new resort in the Bay Area. California retirees and persons looking to escape the pressures of high-tech jobs in the Silicon Valley make up a large component of the inn's business.

Smith has lived in Ashland for more than four decades, and is adept at making everyone feel at home in his inn and his community. The friendly atmosphere is immediately apparent to newly arrived guests, who are affectionately greeted in the main lodge by a supersized, cross-eyed cat named Chester. Grapevine-shaded gazebos, where guests can sit in the afternoon and drink a glass of wine, flank the lodge. Paths from the gazebos lead to the individual cottages.

Most of the cottages contain two-person whirlpool baths that can be filled with slightly sulphurous mineral water. The thermal water leaves a very soft and silky feel to the skin. One couple wrote in the guest book that the mineral-water whirlpool enhanced their "carnal knowledge" during their stay. Another guest, a photographer from Finland, praised the curative effects of the water. The photographer had suffered a rash on her nose since childhood, but after four days of soaking in the mineral water at the inn, the rash disappeared. According to the proprietor the woman carried two gallons of the mineral water with her on the plane home to Finland.

Lithia Springs Inn offers a full breakfast with freshly baked pastries and one or two special main dishes, as well as an assortment of juices, teas, and cereals. All the herbs and many of the vegetables included in the breakfast entrees are raised in the garden behind the inn.

Lithia Springs Inn.

Although the inn doesn't offer lunch or dinner service, nearby Ashland features more than a dozen top restaurants. Inn proprietor Duane Smith is a true aficionado of Ashland's restaurant scene and notes with pride that he has sampled Ashland's best cuisine "more than 500 or 600 times" in the past thirty years. Smith prepares an annual review of Ashland's top restaurants and gladly shares this information with his guests.

Area attractions: In the early twentieth century, the Ashland area was famous for its many mineral and hot springs resorts. A 1935 county directory touted the curative effects of these waters:

> Ashland is famous for its mineral waters. Foremost among these is the Lithia Water—a mineral water that has gained for Ashland the name of "Lithia City." Famed for its curative powers, it is also a delightful beverage and made available in hotels and fountains, the chilled Lithia Water becomes one of the big attractions of the "Lithia City." People suffering from rheumatism, stomach, liver, intestinal and other ailments come from all parts of America for treatment and baths.

Ashland still offers "lithia water" at the public fountain near the hundred-acre Lithia Park. Like all of Ashland's downtown attractions, the park is easily accessible from Lithia Springs Inn via a 2-mile-long bicycle and walking path. Ashland is well known for the Oregon Shakespeare Festival, which attracts more than 400,000 playgoers during its nine-month season.

Kah-Nee-Ta Resort

Contact information:
Kah-Nee-Ta Resort
P. O. Box K
Warm Springs, OR 97761
(541) 553–1112, (800) 554–4SUN (4786)
www.kah-nee-taresort.com

General description: A full-service resort that includes a family-oriented recreation complex, spa facilities, a golf course, a casino, and overnight accommodations ranging from teepees to a 136-room lodge.

Location: Central Oregon, 120 miles east of Portland on the Warm Springs Indian Reservation.

Development: The hot springs have been commercially developed since 1964. In 1972 the lodge was added, and the Indian Head Casino opened in 1995.

Best times to visit: The resort is open year-round. Summer and holidays are especially popular, and the lodge and camping areas are often reserved weeks in advance. Memorial Day to Labor Day is favored by families who stay at the Kah-Nee-Ta village recreation complex. (More than 3,000 vacationers filled the swimming pool on a recent Fourth of July weekend.) During winter months the Kah-Nee-Ta lodge and the Indian Head Casino tend to attract a more mature crowd, who come for the gambling and fine dining.

Kah-Nee-Ta Resort established a marketing office in Portland to entice the urban crowd. One advertising campaign stressed the 300 days of sunshine that Kah-Nee-Ta receives annually. Magazine ads urged rain-weary Portland residents to drive from "drizzle to sizzle in less than two hours."

Call well in advance to reserve rooms in the lodge or teepees in the family village, especially during the summer high season.

Kah-Nee-Ta Resort

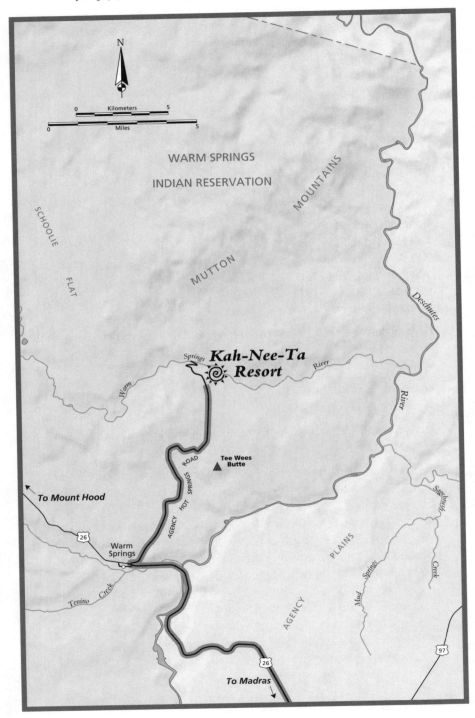

Restrictions: Swimsuits are required in the swimming pools and hot tubs. Guests staying in resort accommodations have free use of the pool; day visitors must pay a small fee. No pets are allowed in the guest rooms.

Access: All roads to Kah-Nee-Ta are paved, so any vehicle can make the trip.

Water temperature: The natural hot springs flow at 130° F. The water is mixed with water from a cooler source to reduce the temperature to a comfortable level in the hot tubs, swimming pool, and spa. The Olympic-sized swimming pool is kept at 86° F. in summer and 92° F. in winter.

Services: Restaurants, lodging, and a wide variety of recreational activities are available at the resort. A small grocery store is located next to the spa. Gasoline can be purchased in Warm Springs, 10 miles south of the resort.

Accommodations: Kah-Nee-Ta Resort has a range of accommodations that will suit everyone's budget and desires. The arrow-shaped Kah-Nee-Ta lodge sits on a ridge about a quarter mile from the village and offers a commanding view of the Warm Springs River and surrounding hills. The lodge features 139 rooms, fine dining, and a private swimming pool.

More casual accommodations are located at Kah-Nee-Ta village, about a quarter mile from the lodge. The village features thirty-one motel rooms, an RV park with fifty-one spots, and twenty authentic Native American teepees. The canvas teepees are especially popular with large families. Each teepee contains a barbecue pit and a picnic table, as well as space for sleeping up to ten. Bring your own sleeping bags and air mattresses to ensure a comfortable night on the teepees' concrete floor.

Map: Oregon State Highway Map.

Finding the springs: From Portland drive 110 miles east on OR 26 through the Oregon Cascades to the town of Warm Springs. On the outskirts of the town of Warm Springs, turn north at the Kah-Nee-Ta sign onto Agency Hot Springs Road and drive 10 miles to the resort.

Overview: Kah-Nee-Ta Resort features one of the largest varieties of recreational activities of any resort in Oregon and Washington. The Kah-Nee-Ta village, next to Warm Springs River, is the focus of most family-oriented activities. Natural hot spring water flows into the Olympic-sized swimming pool, advertised as "Central Oregon's Largest Pool." The warm-water pool contains a 140-foot-long waterslide, which is usually packed with children from the reservation as well as with vacationing visitors. Two communal hot tubs flank the pool, and a wide deck surrounding the pool offers plenty of opportunities for sunbathers.

The 140-foot-long water slide in the Kah-Nee-Ta swimming pool.

Spa Wanapine, the "Spa by the River," is adjacent to the swimming pools. The spa offers a variety of massage treatments, including Swedish massage, deep muscle massage, and reflexology. Two house-special massages are offered: The first starts with a soak in a private tub of natural hot spring water, followed by a full body massage; the second incorporates polished river rocks that are heated in the hot springs and then applied during the massage to help loosen tight muscles. Spa visitors can also choose a variety of facials, body wraps, aromatherapies, and hot mineral-water soaks.

Across an access road behind the spa is an old cement foundation that encloses the original hot springs. A wrought-iron fence encloses this area, but you can still observe the 130° F. water bubbling gently from the rocky bottom of the 15- by 30-foot pool.

Several hot springs farther upstream on the banks of the Warm Springs River are on private reservation land. Off-limits to visitors, these springs are used exclusively by tribal members.

Guests can enjoy many other recreational activities besides soaking and swimming in Kah-Nee-Ta's thermal waters. A section of the Warm Springs River has been reserved for trout fishing (you can purchase a tribal fishing license for $4.00 a day). The resort's 18-hole golf course stays open year-round due to the balmy weather and 300 days of annual sunshine. River trips in inflatable kayaks can be arranged, as can horseback rides. There are several hiking trails into the hills behind the resort (pick up a geology and plant guide of the area at the front desk of the resort).

For guests who desire a sophisticated respite at the end of the day, the Kah-Nee-Ta lodge features the Juniper Room, one of the region's best restaurants. The restaurant's signature dinner entree is the Bird-in-Clay, a stuffed Cornish game hen coated with a layer of clay and then baked in an oven. The clay surrounding the stuffed fowl hardens in the oven's heat, sealing in moisture as the bird slowly bakes. When the dish is brought to the table, guests are given a wooden mallet to crack open the clay shell, releasing the wonderful aromas and savory meat.

The Juniper Room also features a variety of Native American and Pacific Northwest specialties, including salmon and wild game. During summer the resort sponsors a traditional salmon bake on the lawn in front of the lodge. Native Americans dressed in authentic costumes perform traditional dances while the salmon bakes over an alderwood fire.

History: Kah-Nee-Ta Resort probably would not exist today if it weren't for the tragic loss of traditional Native American fishing grounds on the Columbia River. For generations tribal members from the Warm Springs Reservation had fished the Columbia River near Celilo Falls. In 1958 a hydroelectric dam was built across the Columbia River near The Dalles. The water rising behind the dam submerged Celilo Falls, ending the productive salmon fishing that the tribes had depended on for their livelihoods. To compensate the tribes for the loss of their historic fishing grounds, the federal government paid them a lump sum of $4 million. The tribal council gave Oregon State University $100,000 to conduct an economic-development study to determine how to invest this windfall. The analysis recommended that the tribe develop a resort based around the hot springs on the banks of the Warm Springs River.

The tribes took the recommendations to heart. The Kah-Nee-Ta village was completed in 1964, and the Kah-Nee-Ta lodge was opened in 1972. Both the lodge and village proved to be good investments, generating revenue and creating much-needed jobs for tribal members.

In 1996 disaster struck the family resort when a large flood on Warm Springs River destroyed most of the facilities. The resort closed for a year to rebuild, this time incorporating flood-control dikes along the riverbanks. The Spa Wanapine was added to the resort during this reconstruction, which was completed in 1998. The resort began aggressively marketing the rebuilt facilities, and now the Kah-Nee-Ta village and lodge make up the largest revenue source on the Warm Springs Reservation.

Area attractions: Spend an afternoon visiting the Museum at Warm Springs, 10 miles south of the resort. The 25,000-square-foot museum features the great cultural history of the Wasco, Warm Springs, and Paiute tribes that compose the Warm Springs Reservation. The museum features more than 20,000 Native American artifacts, as well as replicas of a tule-mat lodge and a plankhouse. Recorded songs of the three tribes play in the background. An exhibition of salmon fishing and berry gathering gives visitors a sense of tribal life from years gone by.

18

Summer Lake Hot Springs

Contact information:
Summer Lake Hot Springs
28513 Highway 31
Paisley, OR 97636
(541) 943–3931 or (877) 492–8554
www.summerlakehotsprings.com

General description: A hot-water plunge enclosed in an old metalclad barn that's changed little in seventy years. Quirky overnight accommodations and an isolated location add to the resort's charm.

Location: South-central Oregon, 51 miles northwest of Lakeview.

Development: A rustic bathhouse built in the 1920s encloses the hot spring pool. The 143-acre property contains RV and camping spots, a guest house, and vintage Airstream trailers available for overnight rental.

Best times to visit: February and March are peak months for viewing migrating snow geese on nearby Summer Lake. In midsummer hang-gliding aficionados launch from nearby Winter Ridge, some 4,000 feet higher than the surrounding valley, and land on the hot springs property. Stargazers who come to view meteor showers streaking across the night skies prefer autumn. Summer is probably the slowest season at the springs, especially when the heat of July and August make a hot soak less desirable. The resort is especially busy in fall during deer-hunting season.

Restrictions: A fee is charged for day use of the hot springs. Soaking is free to overnight guests. Swimsuits are required in the pool.

Access: Any vehicle can make the trip to Summer Lake Hot Springs, which is located just off OR 31. The resort is open year-round.

Summer Lake Hot Springs

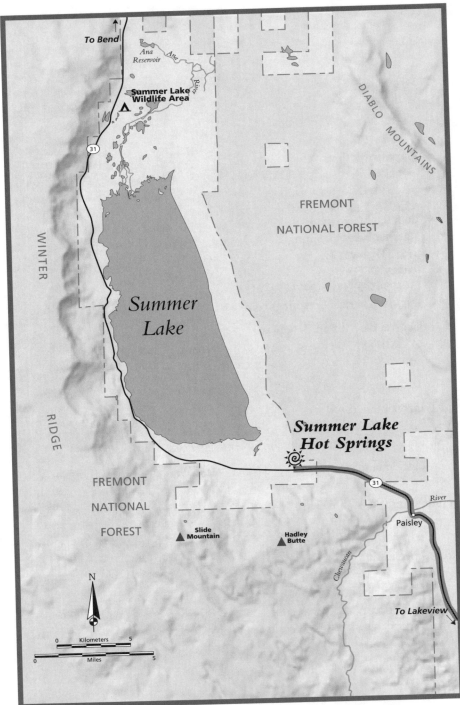

Water temperature: Three separate hot springs, averaging 113° F., are piped to the bathhouse, private hot tubs, and RV-park hookups. A nearby cold spring is piped to the bathhouse for cold showers. The swimming pool in the bathhouse is maintained at a comfortable 102° F. in winter and 98° to 100° F. in summer. The water temperature in the private hot tubs behind the guest house can be adjusted as desired.

Services: No services are available other than lodging, soaking, and enjoying nature. Bring your own food and beverages if you're spending the night at the campground, in one of the vintage Airstream trailers, or in the guest house. You can pick up provisions in Paisley, 6 miles south of the hot springs.

Accommodations: Summer Lake Hot Springs has a variety of lodging options, including eight tent sites (complete with picnic tables made from giant recycled spools that once held telephone wire), sixteen RV sites with full hookups, a two-bedroom guest house that sleeps six, and seven vintage Airstream trailers available for overnight rental. The 1940s-era trailers are furnished with bedding, dishes, a refrigerator, and a stove. They are a very popular lodging option, so it's wise to call ahead to reserve these units. Camping is also available at the Summer Lake Wildlife Area, 22 miles north of the hot springs on OR 31.

Map: Oregon State Highway Map.

Finding the springs: From Lakeview, drive 22 miles north on OR 395 to the junction with Highway 31. Turn left onto OR 31 and drive 23 miles northwest to the small town of Paisley. Drive beyond Paisley for 6 miles on OR 31 to Mile Marker 92, and turn at the Summer Lake Hot Springs sign into the resort driveway.

Overview: One visitor in the 1970s likened the barnlike building that encloses the hot-water pool to "an overgrown chicken coop." The cavernous structure is dimly lit through windows on the west end of the building, and shafts of sunlight that penetrate cracks in the corrugated-steel roof dance on the surface of the warm-water pool.

The 15-foot by 30-foot pool ranges from 3.5 to 5 feet in depth. About twenty gallons per minute of 113° F. hot water is piped into one end of the pool, where it mixes with colder well water to create a comfortable soaking temperature. The pool is flanked by white wooden dressing rooms (men on one side, women on the other). A sagging volleyball net stretched across the center of the pool and a basketball hoop on a side wall provide recreational options for the younger crowd.

History: Explorer John C. Frémont ventured into the valley surrounding the hot springs in 1843 during a reconnaissance expedition to establish a route for the Oregon Trail. Noting the balmy climate of the area, Frémont coined the name

The bathhouse at Summer Lake Hot Springs, little changed since 1927.

Summer Lake for the shallow body of water north of the hot springs. Many settlers soon followed in Frémont's footsteps, most continuing on west but some staying in the sunny valley. By 1873 the town of Paisley, 6 miles south of the hot springs, had its own post office.

Old legends tell of arthritic neighbors being carried by wagon to the undeveloped hot springs where they soaked in the surrounding hot, black mud to alleviate their aches and pains.

The first individual to exploit the economic potential in the hot water was Jonas Woodward, who owned the property in the early 1900s. Woodward carved bathtubs out of large logs that he then filled with hot water for private baths. A wood-lined swimming pool and wooden bathhouse eventually replaced the log tubs. In the early 1920s George Minton purchased the hot springs from the Woodward family. In 1928 Minton's son Claude replaced the original wooden bathhouse with a concrete pool and the corrugated-steel bathhouse. This barn-shaped structure, complete with a pitched roof and gables that let the steam escape from the pool, has welcomed bathers for more than half a century.

In the mid-1930s the Mintons sold the well-known little resort. The hot springs had several owners until the late 1950s, when Jeff McDaniel purchased the property. The springs grew in popularity during the forty years that the McDaniel family managed the hot springs. Jeff McDaniel stated in a 1970s news article that the old hot-water plunge had so many summer visitors that "there's sometimes no place to wiggle a toe." The McDaniel family operated the hot springs resort until 1997, when they sold the property to current owners Duane Graham and Suzy Vitello.

Area attractions: The nearby town of Paisley hosts a Mosquito Festival every summer (bring your own bug repellent). Summer Lake Wildlife Area, located 22 miles north of Summer Lake Hot Springs on OR 31, is an ideal place to spend a spring day watching migrating waterfowl. Hart Mountain National Antelope Refuge lies about 50 miles east of Summer Lake. The Chewaucan River, which flows next to the Paisley, is well known to area fishermen, as are the nearby Sycan, Sprague, and Ana Rivers. Ancient rock drawings can be seen at Picture Rock Pass, about 30 miles north of the hot springs.

19

Geyser (Hunter's) Hot Springs Resort

Contact information:
Geyser Hot Springs Resort
U.S. Highway 395 North
Lakeview, OR 97630
(541) 947–4142 or (877) 686–9889

General description: A motel and restaurant with an outdoor thermal soaking pool. The resort is widely known for its man-made geyser, which has erupted without fail for close to eighty years.

Location: South-central Oregon, 2 miles north of Lakeview on US 395.

Development: The resort has been developed since the early 1900s.

Best times to visit: Geyser Hot Springs is open year-round. Crisp autumn days are a good time to visit to see flocks of migrating birds that stop at the ponds near the resort.

Restrictions: Swimsuits are required in the warm-water pool. Resort guests swim for free; others must pay a day-use fee.

Access: Any vehicle can travel the paved highway to the resort. The outdoor pool is open daily from 10:00 A.M. to 10:00 P.M., but is closed Tuesday evening after 8:00 P.M. for cleaning.

Water temperature: The hot water flows into the open-air swimming pool at a scalding 185° F, but two hoses supply cold water, which keeps the pool at a comfortable 95° to 100° F.

Geyser (Hunter's) Hot Springs Resort

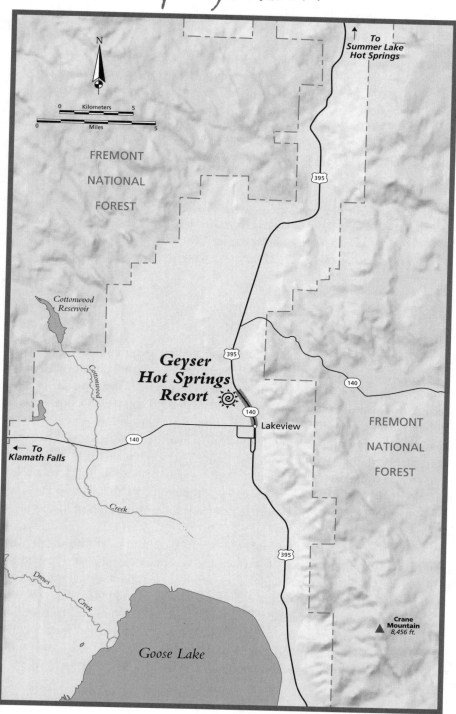

N

0 Kilometers 5

0 Miles 5

FREMONT

NATIONAL

FOREST

Cottonwood
Reservoir

Cottonwood

**Geyser
Hot Springs
Resort**

Lakeview

← **To
Klamath Falls**

140

140

140

395

395

395

↑ **To
Summer Lake
Hot Springs**

140

FREMONT

NATIONAL

FOREST

Creek

Drews

Creek

▲ **Crane
Mountain**
8,456 ft.

Goose Lake

Services: The resort features a restaurant, a lounge, geyser observation, and bird-watching. Gas, groceries, and more restaurant options are available in Lakeview, 2 miles south of the resort.

Accommodations: The current owners of Geyser Hot Springs have done major remodeling of the old resort since they acquired the property in the spring of 2000. Twenty of the old motel rooms have been nicely refurbished and come complete with cable television and telephones. The rooms would make a nice base of operations if you have a long weekend—stay at the resort in the evenings and conduct day trips to nearby Summer Lake Hot Springs and Antelope Hot Springs. An RV park is adjacent to the resort.

Map: Oregon State Highway Map.

Finding the springs: From downtown Lakeview drive north 2 miles on US 395. You'll see the resort just off the highway to the left. Turn at the GEYSER/HUNTER'S HOT SPRINGS sign and park by the main lodge. (Even though the name of the resort was officially changed to Geyser Hot Springs Resort, most locals still refer to it as Hunter's Hot Springs.)

Overview: Just north of the main lodge sits a shallow pond containing the main attraction at Geyser Hot Springs. "Old Perpetual" is a man-made geyser that has erupted regularly for over seventy-five years. (The geyser is "man-made" because it erupts from a well drilled in 1923.) The geyser erupts about every forty seconds, although during extremely dry years or during heavy irrigation of nearby fields, the water table can drop, extending the time between eruptions to up to two minutes. The eruption lasts only about five seconds, so you'll have to move fast if you want to take a picture. The height of the eruption is about 40 feet—much less than the 80-foot to 150-foot eruptions of Old Faithful in Yellowstone Park, but impressive nonetheless. Ducks and geese crowd the warm waters of the ponds in fall and winter.

A neighbor tells an interesting story about Goldfish Lake, the warm-water pool surrounding the geyser. A few years ago an owner of the resort stocked the pool with exotic Japanese koi, which grew quite large in the thermal waters. One autumn a migrating flock of pelicans landed on the pool and proceeded to devour the entire population of expensive fish, much to the chagrin of the resort owner.

Fortunately for resort guests there's another source of thermal water besides the geyser in Goldfish Lake. A separate well supplies 185° F. water to a swimming pool behind the main lodge. The pool is 15 feet by 30 feet and varies from 3 to 5

"Old Perpetual" Geyser at Geyser Hot Springs.

feet deep. Hot water enters through a hose in the pool's deep end. Two other hoses supply cold water to keep the pool at a comfortable temperature.

History: In 1832 a trapper for the Hudson's Bay Company discovered the hot springs. In his journal he described the steaming water: "There is a hot spring in the valley a little to the side of the trail. Some of the young men went to it, and found the water so hot that the finger can barely endure in it a moment. There are a number of human skulls and other bones in it but how they came there is no knowing."

There is little recorded history about the hot springs for the next eighty years, until a wealthy land developer from Minneapolis named Harry Hunter visited the area in 1919. Hunter had traveled through Boise, Idaho, on his trip west and had seen hot springs used to heat buildings in that city. When Hunter saw the hot springs north of Lakeview, he realized the commercial potential of developing the property. Hunter purchased the hot springs in 1923 and began plans to build a sanatorium, a public swimming pool, and a golf course.

The flow of the artesian hot springs wasn't sufficient to supply enough thermal water for Hunter's visions, so he hired a well-drilling company to try to find more hot water. Three wells were drilled in 1923, and to Hunter's surprise they not only found hot water, but all three wells erupted as man-made geysers. Eventually two of the wells died down, but the third well, which was named "Old Perpetual," has continued to erupt to this day.

Hunter was elated with the amount of hot water he found, so he set about to raise capital to build his resort. The experienced developer formed the Hunter's Chlorine Hot Springs Club as a business entity, sold common stock, and raised $100,000 for construction. Hunter built a twenty-two-room sanatorium with an indoor pool for patients and an outdoor pool for recreational use by vacationers. Hot water from one of the wells was used to heat the building, but the geyser was left untouched so that visitors could enjoy its constant display.

Unfortunately Hunter died six years after purchasing the property, and the assets of his Hunter's Chlorine Hot Springs Club were soon liquidated. Over the next seventy years, the resort had a variety of owners. Terry Freeman acquired the property in May of 2000 and is in the process of revitalizing the old resort with a new restaurant and expanded lodging facilities.

Area attractions: Backpackers and mountain bikers can take advantage of the nearby Crane Mountain National Recreational Trail, a scenic 31-mile-long ramble off OR 140 that extends south to the Oregon/California border. Five miles east of Lakeview is Black Cap Overlook, which rises 2,000 feet above the city. Black Cap is a favorite hang-gliding launching area. Warner Canyon Ski Area is about a ten-minute drive east of the hot springs on OR 140.

Antelope (Hart Mountain) Hot Springs

Contact information:
Hart Mountain National Antelope Refuge
Fish and Wildlife Service
National Wildlife Refuge System
18 South G Street
P.O. Box 111
Lakeview, OR 97630–0107
(541) 947–3315
www.recreation.gov/detail.cfm?ID=(1421)

General description: A high-elevation, primitive hot spring located in the center of the Hart Mountain National Antelope Refuge.

Location: South-central Oregon, 68 miles northeast of Lakeview.

Development: Hot water bubbles into a natural rock soaking pool. Crude cinder-block walls and a cement deck detract from the natural beauty of the springs, eliminating what would have been a lovely view of the surrounding meadow.

Best times to visit: Situated just shy of 6,000 feet in elevation, Antelope Hot Springs is best visited in summer and autumn, as winter snow can linger well into spring. The hot springs are especially popular on weekends, holidays, and during fall hunting season, but midweek visitors will rarely find a crowd.

Restrictions: A hand-painted sign on the bathhouse door requests that soaks be limited to twenty minutes when others are waiting and that visitors MUST LOCK DOOR IF NUDE. In practice it seems rare that anyone actually locks the door when soaking in the buff, unless a couple desires privacy. It's probably best to holler before entering the bathhouse to see if it's occupied.

Antelope (Hart Mountain) Hot Springs

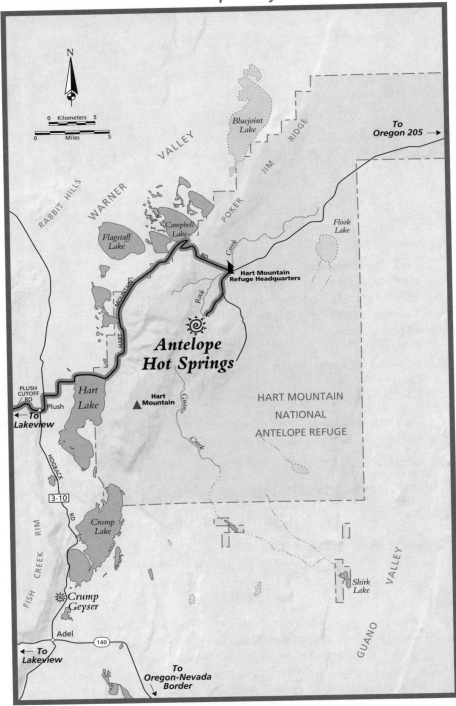

Access: Most vehicles can drive the 65 miles from Lakeview to the refuge head-quarters, although the last 3 or 4 miles switchback more than 2,000 feet up a narrow road to the refuge plateau. The 4-mile road from the refuge headquarters to Antelope Hot Springs is bumpy and poorly maintained, and RV and trailer use is not recommended. Winter snows can sporadically close the road to the hot springs from October through May, although the main refuge road remains open year-round.

Water temperature: The temperature varies between 99° and 102° degrees F. in the soaking pool.

Services: None at the springs, except for a nearby pit toilet. Bring plenty of water and food if you're visiting for the day, and bring all needed camping gear for overnight stays.

Accommodations: Camping accommodations only. The hot soaking pool is surrounded by Hot Springs Campground. No camping permits are required here, but it's still wise to stop at the refuge headquarters to check on current conditions before driving the final 4 miles to the hot springs. The campground has more than a dozen primitive camping spots but no drinking-water source (fill up your water bottles at a spigot near the refuge headquarters building). There's a fourteen-day limit on overnight camping. Camping is also allowed elsewhere on the refuge (especially during special refuge hunting seasons), but a camping permit must be purchased at the refuge headquarters. Backpackers on overnight trips must also obtain a camping permit.

Map: Hart Mountain National Antelope Refuge Recreational Use Map.

Finding the springs: Most visitors to Hart Mountain Antelope Refuge drive northeast from Lakeview. From Lakeview head north 40 miles on OR 395 to the town of Plush. Drive 1 mile north of Plush, then turn east at the sign to Hart Mountain. Follow the signs along Hart Mountain Road about 20 miles to the base of the Hart Mountain escarpment. The road then gains more than 2,000 feet as it switchbacks over the next 3 miles up the side of Hart Mountain to the high-altitude plateau. The refuge headquarters will appear soon after you emerge on the plateau. Stop at the refuge headquarters for the latest information on the hot springs and campground conditions, then proceed to the junction just west of the headquarters. Turn south on the unimproved road to the Hot Springs Campground and drive about 4 miles to the campground and hot springs.

Overview: Situated near the head of Rock Creek in an aspen-dotted meadow, Antelope Hot Springs is a relaxing soak for up to half a dozen people. The soaking pool is about 5 feet deep and 9 feet by 12 feet across. Hot water averaging 100° F.

Soaking pool at Antelope Hot Springs.

bubbles gently from the natural sand-and-rock bottom. A small ladder at one end of the pool provides a way to ease yourself into the warm water (be careful—the wooden stairs can be slippery). A small sitting bench next to the surrounding cinder-block walls provides a place for your clothes. The 8-foot-high walls provide privacy and protection from winter winds but also block any view of the surrounding meadows and hills. Fortunately there's no roof over the hot springs, so it's a great place for stargazing on a clear night.

History: Rumor has it that the springs were first "developed" by a rancher who placed a stick of dynamite in the crack where the original artesian hot springs emerged from the ground. The resulting explosion created the current soaking pool.

Soon after the creation of the Hart Mountain National Antelope Refuge in the 1930s, a citizens' group was formed to provide volunteer assistance. Called the Order of the Antelope, the group helped remove old barbed-wire fences that were a danger to the free-roaming antelope herds. In the late 1930s the Order of the Antelope also constructed the cement-block bathhouse that still surrounds Antelope Hot Springs. Although the Order of the Antelope provided many volunteer services to the refuge, its social events eventually took on a higher priority. By the 1960s the group's annual three-day meeting on the refuge was known more for its wild parties than for any volunteer work. The governor of Oregon finally ordered the removal of the buildings that the Order had constructed for its annual gatherings, and in 1992 the Order of the Antelope ceased its association with the refuge.

Area attractions: The 275,000-acre Hart Mountain National Antelope Refuge surrounding the hot springs provides browse for pronghorn antelope herds in spring and summer. The current antelope population, numbering around 1,200 animals, migrates south and east to lower elevations in the winter months. Since its creation, the refuge has broadened its mission to include conservation of other wildlife and native-plant species.

The refuge sits atop a massive fault block ridge that rises abruptly more than 3,600 feet from the floor of the Warner Valley. Bighorn sheep inhabit many of the rocky crags along the west side of the refuge. The ridge slopes gently to the east, past the refuge headquarters and on more than 40 miles to OR 205. Much of the plateau consists of sagebrush flats that stretch to the horizon. Animals common to the refuge include coyote, deer, and more than 200 species of birds. It's not uncommon to see a dozen or more pronghorn antelopes near the road that bisects the eastern portion of the refuge. One of the swiftest animals on earth, pronghorns can easily reach a speed of 60 miles an hour, much faster than you could possibly drive on the rough washboard road on the plateau. If you are traveling east from the refuge headquarters, leave your speeding antelope fantasies behind and allow a couple of hours to drive the bumpy 40 miles to OR 205.

In addition to wildlife watchers, the refuge is popular with backpackers, fishermen, and hunters. Collecting rock specimens is also a popular activity. The refuge allows rockhounds to collect up to seven pounds of rocks per person per day.

Crump Geyser

Contact information: None available.

General description: A slumbering hot-water well that was at one time the site of the largest continuously erupting geyser in the United States.

Location: South-central Oregon, 3 miles north of Adel.

Development: The well is the only development on the barren hillside over-looking Crump Lake and the Warner Valley.

Best times to visit: Although the well that produces Crump Geyser has a fasci-nating history, it's probably not worth a special trip just to see an enclosed well-head. Nevertheless, if you're visiting Hart Mountain Antelope Refuge or Geyser Hot Springs in Lakeview, consider looping south through the Warner Valley to take a look at the well.

Restrictions: No trespassing signs are posted on the fence enclosing the Crump Geyser. You can park your car about 50 yards from the well but can approach no closer.

Access: Any vehicle can drive on paved CR 3-10 to see the hot-water well.

Water temperature: The water temperature in the well is 220° to 230° F.

Services: None available at the geyser. Drive 3.3 miles south to Adel for food and water at the Adel Restaurant. All other services are available in Lakeview.

Accommodations: Drive north on CR 3-10 through Warner Valley to the Hart Mountain Antelope Refuge for overnight camping and RV spots (as well as a soak in Antelope Hot Springs). Other accommodations are available in Lakeview.

Map: Oregon State Highway Map.

Finding the geyser: From Lakeview drive north for 4 miles on US 395 to the junction with OR 140. Turn east onto OR 140 and drive about 30 miles to the

Crump Geyser

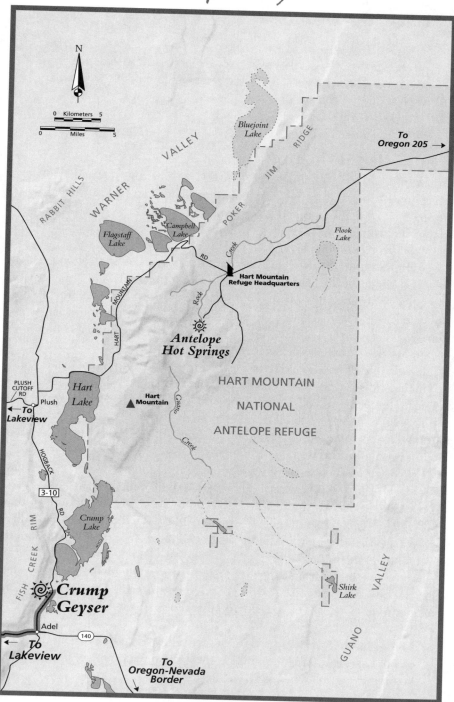

N

0 Kilometers 5
0 Miles 5

RABBIT HILLS

WARNER VALLEY

Bluejoint Lake

POKER JIM RIDGE

To Oregon 205 →

Flagstaff Lake

Campbell Lake

RD

Creek

Flook Lake

Hart Mountain Refuge Headquarters

Rock

HART MOUNTAIN

Antelope Hot Springs

HART MOUNTAIN

NATIONAL

ANTELOPE REFUGE

PLUSH CUTOFF RD

Plush

Hart Lake

▲ Hart Mountain

Guano

Creek

← To Lakeview

HOGBACK RD

3-10

FISH CREEK RIM

Crump Lake

GUANO VALLEY

Shirk Lake

Crump Geyser

Adel

140

← To Lakeview

To Oregon-Nevada Border

small community of Adel. Turn north on CR 3-10 (also called Hogback Road) and drive north for 3.3 miles. On the west side of the road look for a no trespassing sign on a fence. Park your car near the sign. About 50 yards west of the sign, you'll see a mound of earth next to an 8-foot by 8-foot enclosure. Inside the enclosure is the wellhead for Crump Geyser.

About 200 yards east of the well (across the county road) are some small remnants of long-extinct geyser cones and other mineral deposits that indicate geothermal activity in past years.

History: In the early 1950s a rancher named Charles Crump owned 1,300 acres of hay and pastureland in the barren Warner Valley east of Lakeview. In 1959 Crump decided that he needed a new source of irrigation water, so he drilled a well on the west side of the valley. To his surprise the well hit a pocket of hot steam and began erupting every few hours.

Crump was intrigued with the commercial potential of his steaming well; he knew that similar wells has been drilled in California and were being used to power electrical-generation plants. Four years after drilling his initial well, Crump contracted with Magma Power Company of Los Angeles to drill a larger and deeper well near his little geyser, hoping to find 300° F. steam that could power a steam turbine for an electrical generator.

In the summer of 1959, Magma Power arrived at Crump's ranch and drilled a 20-inch-diameter well more than 1,600 feet deep. The drillers recorded water and steam temperatures of 250° F. in the well, but the 1950s technology for converting geothermal steam to electricity required even hotter temperatures (near 300° F.). Disappointed with the water temperature, the energy company removed the drill rig and headed back to California.

Thinking the well was a failure, Crump returned to his ranching. Two days after the well had been abandoned, though, it roared to life, erupting a plume of steam and water that rose more than 150 feet into the air at a continuous volume of 400 and 500 gallons per minute. Unlike the little geyser that Crump had drilled a few years earlier, this new gusher of steam and hot water erupted continuously for more than nine full months.

It must have been an amazing experience to drive through the barren Warner Valley and see the great geyser roaring out of Crump's well. The *Oregonian* sent a reporter in January of 1960 to report on this geologic wonder:

> Nature has her wires crossed in a quiet valley some 30 miles northeast of Lakeview, and the result is a spectacular nightmare of ice and steam that few folks are likely ever to see.

Crump Geyser in 1960.   PHOTO: OREGON STATE UNIVERSITY ARCHIVES

The scene is a small patch of land in a corner of the Warner Valley on the ranch of Charles A. Crump. This is Crump's Geyser, a gusher of water, boiling from the earth at 220 degrees in a stream that spouts 150 feet into the air, at least 30 feet higher than Old Faithful.

The icy wind blowing down from the Warner Rim has caught up the steam, freezing some of it before it hits the ground and creating a three-acre sea of ice that ripples over the field and roadway in one great slippery blanket. Taut fence wire has been crushed to the ground by the heavy sheets of ice built up by the freezing vapor from the geyser, fence posts have been transformed into marblelike columns, almost alive with the layer upon layer of ice built up on the freezing weather.

The geyser may have continued to spout for a very long time, but vandals clogged the well with boulders and rocks in the spring of 1960. The wondrous Crump Geyser has never erupted since.

The story doesn't end there, however. The original irrigation well that Crump had drilled five years earlier had ceased erupting when the massive 1959 geyser had sprung to life. After the vandalism halted the eruption of the new geyser, Crump's "old" geyser began to spout again intermittently, erupting 90 feet into the air every eight to ten hours.

Through the 1960s and 1970s, the "old" geyser continued its infrequent display, but over time the intervals increased between eruptions, and eventually the geyser ceased altogether. As late as the mid-1990s, the Crumps could occasionally force an eruption by lowering a bucket into the well until it filled with water and then retrieving it, an action that disturbed the dynamics of the water pressure just enough to cause the geyser to blow.

Area attractions: CR 3-10 (Hogback Road) continues north past Crump Geyser through the Warner Valley to the town of Plush. The Hart Mountain National Antelope Refuge (which contains Antelope Hot Springs) is about 20 miles northeast of Plush.

Blue Mountain Hot Springs

Contact information:
Blue Mountain Hot Springs
Star Route
Prairie City, OR 97876
(541) 820–3744

General description: A peaceful, warm-water swimming pool on the grounds of a former guest ranch.

Location: Northeast Oregon, 10 miles southeast of Prairie City near the Strawberry Mountain Wilderness.

Best times to visit: The hot springs swimming pool is open year-round. Midweek in autumn and spring may be best if you want to avoid crowds (you may be the only person soaking at this time). Winter is also uncrowded, but occasionally snow will close the road to the springs.

Restrictions: The hot springs are privately owned, and an admission fee is charged to soak and swim in the pool. The pool is open from 10 A.M. to 8 P.M. daily, but is occasionally closed at the owner's discretion and for private family gatherings.

Access: Any vehicle can make the 10-mile trip along the blacktop road from Prairie City to the hot springs.

Water temperature: The hot springs average 136° F, cooling to 120° F. as they enter the swimming pool 10 feet to the north. The temperature of the swimming pool hovers around 100° F.

Services: None at the springs other than showers, a changing room, and a bathroom. Bring a picnic lunch to enjoy on the expansive lawns that stretch between the old Blue Mountain Lodge and the swimming pool.

Blue Mountain Hot Springs

Accommodations: No camping at the hot springs (day-use only). Several campgrounds are nearby, including Depot Park (which is the city park in Prairie City). Depot Park has facilities for both tent camping and RVs. There are also several campgrounds south of Blue Mountain Hot Springs in the Malheur National Forest and Strawberry Mountain Wilderness. Stop at the USFS office in Prairie City for current camping information and regulations. Prairie City also offers more civilized accommodations, including the Riverside Schoolhouse Bed & Breakfast, which is 4 miles north of the hot springs on CR 62 (541–820–4731), and the Strawberry Mountain Inn, which is on the eastern edge of Prairie City (800–545–6913).

Maps: Oregon State Highway Map, USGS Prairie City.

Finding the springs: From US 26 in Prairie City, turn south onto Main Street. Drive 0.3 mile, then turn right onto Bridge Street. Continue south on Bridge Street across the John Day River. Bridge Street then turns into CR 62 (also called the Logan Valley Road). Drive 10 miles southeast on CR 62. Between Mileposts 10 and 11, look for a large black mailbox and a PRIVATE PROPERTY sign on the north side of the road. Turn onto the gravel road by the mailbox and drive about 0.3 mile past an old homestead until you come to the two-story Blue Mountain Lodge. A sign by the parking area will direct you to knock on the hotel door and pay the owner $3.50 for soaking rights in the warm-water swimming pool. After paying your fee, walk downhill about 100 yards to the bathhouse and pool.

Overview: The open-air concrete swimming pool has changed little in the past half century. The pool is about 4 feet deep and measures 30 feet by 70 feet. The actual hot springs bubble into a small basin 10 feet west of the swimming pool on the opposite side of a chain-link fence. Plastic pipes bring the 120° F. natural hot water into the pool. The pool temperature averages about 100° F. The warmest soaking spot is near the concrete steps close to the pipe where the main hot springs enter the pool.

History: The hot springs were first claimed in the 1860s by homesteader John Douglas, who built a log house and an enclosed swimming pool. Blue Mountain Hot Springs became a popular vacation destination, and subsequent owners in the early 1900s built a hotel, a dance hall, a horse stable, a bathhouse, and an icehouse.

E. C. Tuttle purchased the hotel and hot springs in 1945. Tuttle, who made his fortune as an executive with the Winchester Firearms and Ammunition Company, closed the springs to public access. From 1945 until 1965 Tuttle used the property as a private retreat for his family and friends.

Swimming pool at Blue Mountain Springs.

Testimonies abound as to the healing properties of the mineral water at Blue Mountain Hot Springs. In 1945 a construction worker spent five months at the springs, performing carpentry work on Blue Mountain Lodge for the new owner, E. C. Tuttle. More than two decades after his summer at the springs, the construction worker wrote a letter to the current owners of the resort, describing the wonderful benefits he received from the hot springs water:

My Dear Sir:

I am enclosing a picture of the Blue Mountain Lodge as it looked when I arrived there April 18, 1945 and also a picture of the completed work taken on September 20, 1945. Everybody was pleased with outcome including the owner Mr. Tuttle, my boss, Mr. Stanton, the architect and myself as supervising the architects.

You know I received a reward for my part in this work, besides my pay.

When I went up to do this work at Blue Mountain Hot Springs, I didn't feel too good. I had been troubled with arthritis in my hands, feet, legs, arms and shoulder for some time—about eight years or more. I normally weighed 165 pounds and when I went on the job up there I weighed 142 pounds. Anyway, after about six weeks on the job I noticed I was feeling better and my joints didn't hurt as much. I had been drinking the hot water from the spring from then until fall or September. I sure filled up on the hot water and cold water from the irrigation ditch from Rail Creek. I expect I drank about a gallon or more of hot water each day. That fall and before, the swelling in my hand and my hurting joints had all gone away. I helped the care-taker of the ranch split his wood after living there a month. I went home without an ache or pain and I weighed 172 pounds. I have never had any arthritis since—that was my extra pay and bonus. I am grateful that I took on the supervisor's job at the Blue Mountain Hot Springs and I hope some other person with that trouble would try it out. I think it would work even if they didn't have the same kind of arthritis that I had.

Yours truly,
Charles R. Kaufman
Portland, Oregon

Upon Tuttle's death in 1965, Eugene and Helen Ricco purchased Blue Mountain Hot Springs and reopened the swimming pool to the public. The Riccos also reopened the Blue Mountain Lodge and provided room and board to guests. The Ricco family still owns and operates the swimming pool and adjacent ranch, although the hotel is no longer open to the public.

Area attractions: The 1.5 million-acre Malheur National Forest surrounding Blue Mountain Hot Springs is home to many recreational opportunities. The forest offers camping, fishing, snowmobiling, hunting, and other outdoor opportunities. Strawberry Mountain Wilderness attracts backpackers who explore the alpine lakes surrounding the peak of 9,038-foot Strawberry Mountain. Malheur National Forest was in the world spotlight in the late 1990s, when scientists announced that they had discovered the largest organism on earth in the forest near Prairie City. The organism, a subterranean mushroom named *Armillaria ostoyae*, covers an area more than 3 miles across (that's more than 1,500 football fields) and extends an average of 3 feet into the ground. This monster mushroom has probably been growing for close to 2,500 years, slowly extending its filaments through tree roots beneath the forest floor. In autumn small brown mushrooms pop up to the surface after rain showers, but the threadlike filaments that compose the bulk of the organism remain hidden beneath the surface. Scientists from Oregon State University discovered the mushroom after looking at aerial photos of large expanses of trees killed by root rot caused by the mushroom. Stop by the USFS ranger station in Prairie City for more information on this botanical behemoth.

Ritter Hot Springs

Contact information:
Ritter Hot Springs
Box 16
Ritter, OR 97872
(541) 421–3846

General description: A historic overnight stop on the old stagecoach road between Pendleton and John Day.

Location: Northeast Oregon, 90 miles south of Pendleton.

Development: The rustic resort has changed little from the turn of the century. It features an old hotel, a general store, and a warm-water swimming pool.

Best times to visit: Ritter Hot Springs is open Memorial Day to Labor Day; it is closed in the winter months. Resort hours are Sunday to Wednesday from 8:00 A.M. to 10:00 P.M., and Thursday from 8:00 A.M. to 6:00 P.M. The resort is closed Friday and Saturday.

Restrictions: Swimsuits are required in the pool.

Access: Any vehicle can drive to the hot springs on the paved road that parallels the Middle Fork of the John Day River. There's a $2.00 fee charged to swim in the warm-water pool. Regular visitors can buy a season pass for $20.00 or $45.00 for a family of four.

Water temperature: The hot springs emerge from the ground at 106° F. The hot water is piped across the Middle Fork of the John Day River to the swimming pool, which averages 85° F.

Services: A few snacks are available in the old Ritter Springs General Store. Pay for your snacks and your swimming pool fee under the honor system by leaving your cash in the box on a nearby table.

Ritter Hot Springs

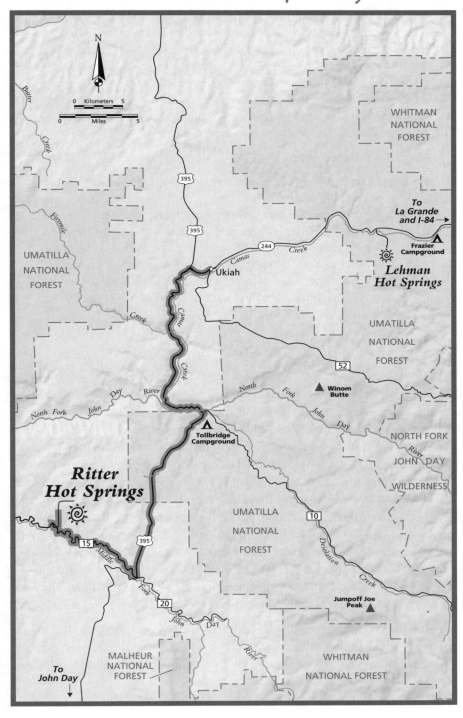

N

0 Kilometers 5

0 Miles 5

WHITMAN
NATIONAL
FOREST

UMATILLA
NATIONAL
FOREST

To
La Grande
and I-84 →

Frazier
Campground

Lehman
Hot Springs

UMATILLA

NATIONAL

FOREST

Ukiah

Winom
Butte

NORTH FORK

JOHN DAY

WILDERNESS

Ritter
Hot Springs

Tollbridge
Campground

UMATILLA

NATIONAL

FOREST

Jumpoff Joe
Peak

MALHEUR
NATIONAL
FOREST

To
John Day
↓

WHITMAN

NATIONAL FOREST

Butter

Creek

Fivemile

Creek

Camas

Creek

Camas

Creek

North Day River

North Fork John

Day River

North   Fork

John   Day

Middle

Fork

John   Day

River

Desolation

Creek

395

395

244

52

10

15

395

20

Accommodations: The historic Ritter Springs Hotel offers eight spartan rooms for about $20 a night. There's a separate bathroom building attached to the hotel. Bring your own food, water, and picnic gear, because there are no supplies or cooking facilities available in the hotel. Next to the hotel are some fire pits and picnic tables that you can use for preparing your meals. Also available are several furnished rental cabins complete with kitchens. It's best to call ahead for reservations, especially if you want to rent one of the rooms in the hotel. RV and camping spots are also available for a small fee.

Another overnight option is Tollbridge USFS campground, 14 miles south of Ukiah on Highway 395, then 1 mile east on Forest Road 10.

Map: Oregon Highway Map.

Finding the springs: From Ukiah head west on OR 244 for 1 mile to US 395. Drive south on US 395 for 39 miles to CR 15. (You'll come to the turnoff just before crossing a bridge over the Middle Fork of the John Day River.) Turn west on CR 15 and check the Ritter Hot Springs information sign near the turnoff to be sure the resort is open. Follow CR 15 west parallel to the Middle Fork of the John Day River for 10 miles. Turn north onto a gravel road marked with a Ritter Hot Springs sign and drive about 1.5 miles. Park your car next to the Ritter Springs General Store. The swimming pool and hotel are both within 100 yards of the parking area.

Overview: Pulling up to the Ritter Springs General Store puts you in company with the thousands of cowboys and settlers who stopped here on the old stagecoach run to Pendleton. The Ritter Stage Road followed winding river valleys and steep ridges, culminating in a steep, 5-mile descent to the Ritter Springs stage stop. Frontier travelers surely welcomed the respite from the harrowing trip provided by the swimming pool and hotel at Ritter Springs.

Present-day visitors delight in the same mineral water and rustic lodging that stagecoach passengers enjoyed one hundred years ago. The 40-foot by 60-foot swimming pool is kept around 85° F., a comfortable temperature for swimming during the May-to-October resort season. For a warmer soak take the footbridge across the Middle Fork of the John Day River to the source of the hot springs. There are four private bathtubs near the springs that can be filled with the 106° F. hot water. Check before using these tubs to be sure that they are available.

History: The hot springs were originally called McDuffie Springs, named for William Neal McDuffie, who discovered them in the early 1880s. Joseph Ritter, a Baptist minister who settled near the hot springs property, established the first

The rustic Ritter Springs Hotel.

post office in the region. The Ritter post office was later moved to the general store at the little resort, and the preacher's name became thereafter linked to the hot springs.

The Ritter Springs Hotel and General Store served as a stagecoach stop on the old Ritter Road between Pendleton and John Day. The general store was built in 1894. A faded sign above the entrance to the store advertises what must have been considered essential supplies to travelers at the turn of the century:

1894—Ritter Springs—1894
General Store & Stage Stop
Ranchers and Cowboys Supplies,
Bull Durham Chawin Tobacco,
45 Colt & Winchester Ammunition
First Aid Kits

The two-story Ritter Springs Hotel was built in 1905. The wooden clapboard building featured eight guest rooms on the first floor. The second floor was used both as a meeting place and a dance hall.

Visitors from as far away as Portland made yearly pilgrimages to soak in the hot springs at Ritter. Local historian Jo Southworth recalled the resort's popularity in a 1972 article in *The Blue Mountain Eagle*:

> In spite of the challenge of reaching Ritter, people went for a day or for weeks. They stayed in the hotel or the cabins, or camped in their own tents. Victims of all types of rheumatism, skin disease, stomach trouble and other ailments sought relief from their afflictions. Some of the inflammatory rheumatism cases came in on stretchers. The grayish green moss that grew in the mineral water helped skin infections when bandaged to the sores. People dried the moss and took it home for further treatment. Stomach patients drank the water. One of them was so miserable he could hardly eat. He was restored to such good health by Ritter Hot Springs treatment that he even enjoyed eating spare ribs with the other diners by the end of the day.

Area attractions: Fishermen are often seen along the Middle Fork of the John Day River. Camping, hiking, and hunting are the main attractions in the Blue Mountains and the North Fork John Day Wilderness east of Toll Bridge Campground.

Lehman Hot Springs

Contact information:
Lehman Hot Springs
Box 187
Ukiah, Oregon 97880
(541) 427–3015
www.lehmanhotsprings.com

General description: A popular mountain resort that features one of the largest pools in the Pacific Northwest.

Location: Northeast Oregon, 38 miles west of La Grande in the Blue Mountains.

Development: First developed in the 1880s as a summer resort, Lehman Hot Springs is now an all-season destination for outdoor enthusiasts.

Best times to visit: The resort is busy throughout the year. Families often rent the large bunkhouse for reunions. Mountain biking is popular in summer, hunters use the resort as a base in fall, and winter brings a migration of snowmobilers and cross-country skiers. Reserve your lodging as far in advance as possible, especially if you're planning to visit during holidays, winter weekends, or the autumn hunting season.

Restrictions: Bathing suits are required in the pools.

Access: Any vehicle can make the trip on the paved highway and gravel road that lead to the hot springs. Accommodations are available seven days a week, but the pools are closed Monday and Tuesday for cleaning and are also closed on Thanksgiving Day, Christmas Eve, and Christmas Day. Pool hours are from 10:00 A.M. to 8:00 P.M. Wednesday through Sunday, with extended hours on the weekends during summer. The cold-water pool is closed (and covered in ice) from November through March.

Lehman Hot Springs

N

0 Kilometers 5
0 Miles 5

UMATILLA
NATIONAL
FOREST

WHITMAN
NATIONAL
FOREST

395

395

*To
La Grande
and I-84* →

244

Camas

Creek

LEHMAN
SPRINGS
RD

Frazier
Campground

Ukiah

*Lehman
Hot Springs*

UMATILLA
NATIONAL
FOREST

52

Winom
Butte

Comas

Creek

North

Fork

John

Day

North Fork

John

Day

River

North Fork

John Day River

Tollbridge
Campground

NORTH FORK

JOHN DAY

WILDERNESS

*Ritter
Hot Springs*

15

395

UMATILLA
NATIONAL
FOREST

10

Middle

Desolation

Creek

20

Fork

John

Day

River

Jumpoff Joe
Peak

MALHEUR
NATIONAL
FOREST

WHITMAN

NATIONAL

FOREST

*To
John Day*
↓

Water temperature: The hot springs average a steamy 168° F. at their source on the hillside above the pools. The thermal-soaking-pool temperatures vary with the season, ranging from 92° to 130° F.

Services: A deli and gift shop are located next to the swimming pools.

Accommodations: Lehman Hot Springs offers a variety of overnight options. The most civilized accommodations include a log cabin that sleeps four and an A-frame house that sleeps eight; the bunkhouse, which holds up to forty-eight, is popular with large groups. There are thirteen RV spaces, with full hookups, overlooking the swimming pool. Tent camping is available in a secluded area near a creek. If you're looking for a unique place to rest your head, consider renting one of the teepees constructed by local Native Americans. Free camping is available at the USFS Frazier Campground, situated 2 miles east of Lehman Hot Springs. To reach the campground drive 2 miles east on OR 244, then turn south onto FR 5226 for 0.5 mile.

Map: Oregon State Highway Map.

Finding the springs: From La Grande drive west on I–84 for 7.5 miles. Turn south onto OR 244. Drive southwest for 30 miles to Milepost 17. Turn south on Lehman Springs Road (CR 917) for 1.5 miles to the hot-springs resort. If you're heading from Ukiah, drive 16 miles east on OR 244 to Milepost 17. Turn south on Lehman Springs Road and then drive 1.5 miles to the hot-springs resort.

Overview: The steaming valley first discovered by James Lehman contains more than fifty separate hot springs that bubble to the surface 500 yards uphill from the swimming pools. The runoff from these springs forms a hot-water creek that flows parallel to a cold-water creek a few feet away. Legend has it that visitors to the hot springs would fish for trout in the cold stream. Upon catching a dinner-sized fish, the angler would swing the hooked fish into the adjacent hot-water creek, where it would cook in a few minutes.

The largest of the many hot springs are collected into pipes that lead downhill to the swimming-pool complex. Hot water first enters the smallest and hottest pool, which reaches a maximum temperature of 130° F. in summer, cooling to around 110° F. in winter. First-time bathers sometimes try to soak in this pool, but it's almost always too hot. The middle pool is a more comfortable106° to 108° F., whereas the lower pool stays between 92° and 96° F. The temperature in the cold-water pool hovers around 55° F. The four pools combined exceed 9,000 square feet, which resort literature claims is the largest swimming-pool complex in the Pacific Northwest.

Lehman Hot Springs, one of the largest soaking pools in the Pacific Northwest.

History: Legend has it that the Umatilla and Cayuse tribes summered in the area near the hot springs to pick huckleberries. James Lehman and Dr. John Teel were the first Europeans to visit the hot springs. While hunting in the area in the fall of 1871, Lehman and Teel followed some deer tracks into a small canyon, where they discovered the steaming hot water. The men camped near the springs overnight, then traveled to Pendleton the next day to file a claim on the land. The hot springs were called "Teel Springs" until the death of Dr. Teel in 1880, when James Lehman became the sole owner and namesake.

Within a few years Lehman turned the natural springs into a popular summer resort, complete with hotel, store, barbershop, dance hall, and swimming pool. According to a history of the resort written by Mildred Searcey, hot mud baths were available in small cabins built next to the pool, where guests would soak in "slimy, gooey mud."

The twenty-eight-room hotel that Lehman built was eventually destroyed by fire, and the other original resort buildings were replaced. Patrick and Rachel Lucas have owned the resort since the early 1990s.

Area attractions: The hot springs are a private inholding surrounded by the Wallowa-Whiteman National Forest. East of the resort, Hilgard State Park offers camping and picnic spots along the banks of the Grande Ronde River. Close by is the Anthony Lakes Mountain Resort, featuring both downhill and cross-country skiing. West of the hot springs, the USFS maintains the Winoma-Frazier Off-Highway Vehicle Complex, which provides motorized-vehicle enthusiasts with more than 100 miles of trails.

Hot Lake Hotel and Sanitarium

Contact information: None available.

General description: An abandoned brick hotel on the shores of a warm-water lake formed by one of Oregon's most historic hot springs.

Location: Northeast Oregon, 8 miles southeast of La Grande in the Grande Ronde Valley.

Development: Hot Lake has been commercially developed since the 1860s. The massive brick hotel has been unoccupied for decades.

Restrictions: No trespassing on the hotel property or bathing in the thermal lake or hot springs.

Access: Although you can't enter the property, you can observe the old hotel and the steaming lake of hot water if you park your car on the side of OR 30 next to the entrance to the hotel. Any vehicle can make the trip on the paved highway.

Water temperature: The hot springs are located in a small building between the lake and the hotel. The artesian hot springs produce 2.5 million gallons per day of 198° F. water.

Services: Gas and food are available in nearby La Grande and Union. A few snacks are available at the Hot Lake RV Resort, 0.5 mile west of the hotel.

Accommodations: Hot Lake RV Resort has more than one hundred spaces for motor homes. A camping area is also provided. Other accommodations are available in La Grande and Union.

Hot Lake Hotel and Sanitarium

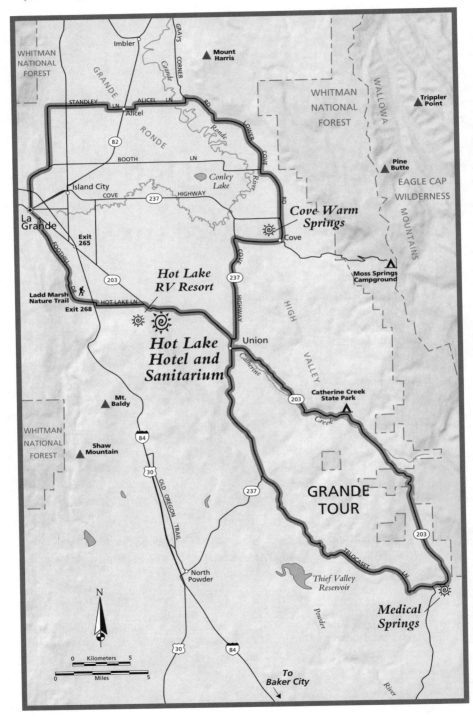

WHITMAN NATIONAL FOREST

Imbler

GRAYS CORNER

Mount Harris

WHITMAN NATIONAL FOREST

WALLOWA

Trippler Point

GRANDE

Grande

STANDLEY LN   ALICEL LN

Alicel

82

RONDE

Ronde

LOWER COVE

River

BOOTH   LN

Conley Lake

Island City

COVE   HIGHWAY   237

Pine Butte

EAGLE CAP WILDERNESS

MOUNTAINS

Cove Warm Springs

Cove

RD

La Grande

Exit 265

FOOTHILL DR

203

Ladd Marsh Nature Trail
Exit 268

HOT LAKE LN

Hot Lake RV Resort

COVE

237

HIGHWAY

Moss Springs Campground

Hot Lake Hotel and Sanitarium

Union

Catherine

HIGH VALLEY

Mt. Baldy

84

WHITMAN NATIONAL FOREST

Shaw Mountain

30

OLD OREGON TRAIL

203

Catherine Creek State Park

Creek

237

GRANDE TOUR

203

North Powder

Thief Valley Reservoir

TELOCASET LN

Medical Springs

N

Powder

0   Kilometers   5
0   Miles   5

30   84

To Baker City

River

Map: Oregon State Highway Map.

Finding the springs: From La Grande, drive south on I–84 for 2.5 miles to exit 265. Take the exit and drive east for 5 miles on OR 203. On the right-hand side of the highway, you'll see the warm-water lake and abandoned brick hotel. Park your car near the locked entrance to the hotel and spend a few minutes looking at the property from the parking area.

Overview and History: Hot Lake was likely the first hot springs in the Pacific Northwest to have been seen by Europeans. Robert Stuart, a member of the Astor Expedition, was returning from the Oregon Coast to St. Louis, Missouri, in the summer of 1812. Stuart's observations were later recorded by writer Washington Irving:

> Emerging from the chain of Blue Mountains, they descended upon a vast plain, almost a dead level, sixty miles in circumference, of excellent soil, with fine streams meandering through it in every direction, their courses marked out in the wide landscape by serpentine lines of cotton-wood trees, and willows, which fringed their banks, and afforded sustenance to great numbers of beavers and otters.
>
> In traversing this plain, they passed, close to the skirts of the hills, a great pool of water, three hundred yards in circumference, fed by a sulphur spring, about ten feet in diameter, boiling up in one corner. The vapor from this pool was extremely noisome, and tainted the air for a considerable distance. The place was much frequented by elk, which were found in considerable numbers in the adjacent mountains, and their horns, shed in the spring-time, were strewed in every direction around the pond.
>
> —from *Astoria: or, Anecdotes of an Enterprise Beyond the Rocky Mountains* (1836)

A few decades after Stuart's visit, pioneers trekked across the Oregon Trail on their way west. The wagon trail passed within sight of Hot Lake, and the pioneers often stopped to rest, wash their clothes, and bathe in the hot water.

Eventually the hot springs and adjacent warm-water lake were incorporated into a surrounding cattle ranch. In 1914 the *Oregonian* recounted a story of one of the early ranch hands who was enamored with the healing properties of Hot Lake:

The abandoned Hot Lake Hotel.

[At one time] Hot Lake was merely part of a ranch occupied by a former sailor named Tommy Atkins. He was most loyal to the curative power of healing Hot Lake, whose boiling, steaming waters had for centuries been the faithful remedy for hosts of Indians from near and far. Tommy swore loudly that the hot water of this odd lake would absolutely cure any human ailment.

Tommy was the proud owner of 30 horses, among which was a young mare, beautiful in form and color, but wild, fiery and unbroken. Tommy swore that he would tame and ride this animal. The result of the first lesson was that the indignant equine pupil hoisted aloft the sailor, then stamped, kicked and bit him. The maimed Tommy was picked up for dead and hauled to his beloved Hot Lake.

He balked at any doctoring, swearing fluently at the medical men's verdict that he had three cracked ribs, a broken arm, fractured leg and sundry serious internal injuries. After nightfall, when the doctors had given up hope and departed, the apparently doomed sailor quietly crawled out to the shore of the lake. With a volley of muttered oaths, he flopped into the steaming water and floundered around like a fish or lobster.

By chance he drifted too near to where the boiling, fiery water laps up from the earth and is 15 feet deep. Too weak to resist, Tommy was drawn into this hissing whirlpool of Hades. His howls, yells, yowls, whoops and gurgling curses brought a neighboring rancher out on the run. The rancher heaved a rope to the flopping, screeching victim and towed the partly cooked, rosy red sailor to the harbor of solid land. Some reports assert that this Tommy Atkins was cured of every ailment, including his swearing habit.

In 1864 a small hotel was built on the property. The hotel was heated with water from the hot springs, one of the first commercial uses of geothermal energy in the United States. Dr. H. J. Minthorn leased the property in 1889, and added two wings to the little hotel. Other new features included a new bathhouse and an octagonal springhouse that enclosed the bubbling hot water.

The resort was expanded again in 1908 with the addition of a 200-foot-long brick hospital with 105 rooms. The new hospital could provide therapeutic mineral-water soaks to more than 200 patients a day in large tiled rooms containing rows of sunken bathtubs. There were also a surgical area (complete with elevated observation area) and a dining hall that could seat 1,500. At its height the hospital was staffed with four physicians, fifteen nurses, an X-ray technician, and a bacteriologist. Other additions soon followed, including a barbershop, a ballroom, a poolroom, bathhouses, a drugstore, a cafeteria, and a hospital. The sheer size and variety of facilities located in the building earned the resort the label "The Town Under One Roof."

The Hot Lake Hospital and Sanitarium was also known as "The Mayo Clinic of the West." A promotional flyer from the regional railroad company extolled the curative properties of the natural hot springs:

> The largest, hottest, and most curative springs known; best bathing facilities, most courteous attendants; first-class medical and surgical conveniences; finest operating room in the west; steam heat, electric lights; hot and cold water throughout the building.

Another advertisement touted the benefits that guests received from bathing in and drinking the hot mineral springs:

> The water, pleasing to the taste, has cured and restored to health innumerable invalids, who had tried in vain much-advertised and noted resorts. The treatments consists of copious drinking of the water, hot-water baths, hot-vapor baths and hot-mud baths—the heat

Sunken hot-water soaking tubs at Hot Lake Sanitarium. PHOTO: COURTESY OREGON HISTORICAL SOCIETY

in all cases being from the water as it comes from the ground. A poultice from the sediment at the bottom of the lake relieves the most agonizing form of rheumatism, and reduces the swelling. Long-standing cases of dyspepsia have been cured by a few weeks' use of the water.

On May 7, 1934, a fire destroyed all the wooden buildings on the property, leaving only the brick hotel. The fireproof building was reopened after the fire, but the resort's popularity never regained the levels seen before the fire. The property changed hands several times over the next fifty years, finally serving as a retirement home in the 1970s. A string of owners in the 1980s and 1990s proposed grand ideas to revitalize the resort to its former glory, but none of these plans ever materialized.

The darkened hotel has become the source of several ghost stories. A caretaker in the 1990s reported hearing a piano playing on the third floor, even though the building was empty. He also heard ghostly screams coming from the old surgery room and observed that three rocking chairs sitting in a row on the third floor "never seem to get dusty," as if somebody or something was sitting in them.

At present even the caretaker is gone, and the Hot Lake Hotel sits abandoned, most of its windows broken by vandals and its once well-manicured lawns overgrown with weeds. The warm water where pioneers washed their clothes 150 years ago is choked with cattails, but the hot springs continue to produce millions of gallons daily of steaming water as they have for thousands of years.

Area attractions: Ladd Marsh, a 3,000-acre wildlife sanctuary, is adjacent to Hot Lake. It's a great place to spend a few hours observing dozens of species of waterfowl. There's a nature trail through the sanctuary.

Hot Lake is on the 95-mile-long, figure-eight Grande Tour from La Grande through Hot Lake and on to Union and Medical Springs. From Medical Springs the driving tour then heads back to Union and north to Cove before returning to La Grande. This is a nice daylong tour if you're staying in La Grande. Pick up a tour map and area-highlight descriptions at the La Grande/Union County Visitors and Convention Bureau.

Hot Lake RV Resort

Contact information
Hot Lake RV Resort
65182 Hot Lake Lane
La Grande, OR 97850
(541) 963–5253 or (800) 994–5253

General description: A pleasant overnight spot for the Winnebago crowd, complete with a natural hot springs pool.

Location: Northeast Oregon, 8 miles southeast of La Grande in the Grande Ronde Valley.

Restrictions: The mineral-water soaking pools are open from 10:00 A.M. to 9:00 P.M. The pools are available to registered resort guests only. No campfires are allowed.

Access: Any vehicle can make the trip.

Water temperature: The two soaking pools average 100° F.

Services: Snack bar, groceries, laundry, showers, and rest rooms.

Map: Oregon State Highway Map.

Finding the springs: From La Grande drive south on I–84 for 2.5 miles to exit 265. Take the exit and drive east for 5 miles on OR 203. Turn right (east) onto Hot Lake Lane, just before the abandoned Hot Lake Hotel. Drive 0.5 mile on this gravel road to the RV resort, on the left-hand side of the road.

You can also reach the resort from La Grande by driving 5.5 miles south on I–84 to exit 268, then go west on Hot Lake Lane for 1.5 miles to the resort.

Hot Lake RV Resort

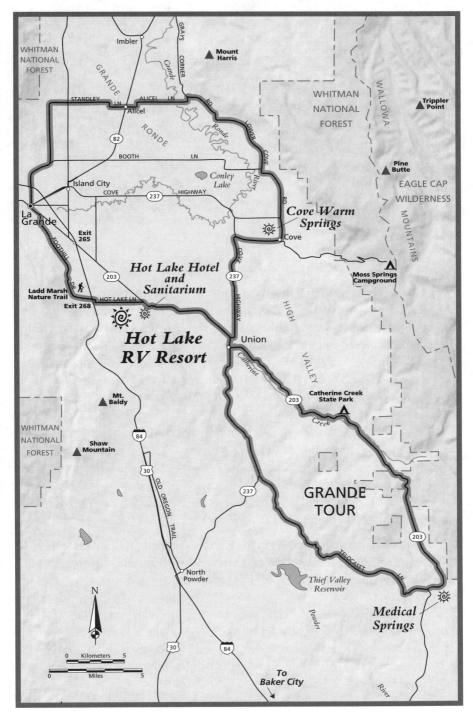

The natural hot-water soaking pool at Hot Lake RV Resort.

Overview: Located less than half a mile from the abandoned Hot Lake Hotel, the thirty-acre Hot Lake RV Resort opened in the late 1980s. The resort is a well-known stop for motor-home tourists passing through the Grande Ronde Valley. More than a hundred full-service RV pull-thrus are available, as well as a separate creekside camping area shaded by willow and cottonwood trees. A picnic area is also located near the creek. The resort features a private bass fishing pond and stream—resort guests can try their luck without needing a fishing license.

The main lodge contains a small grocery store, a laundry area, and showers. The walls of the lodge are lined with large black-and-white photos of nearby Hot Lake Hotel during its heyday in the 1920s.

Behind the lodge are two natural hot-water soaking pools, supplied with 160° F. water from a nearby well. The largest soaking pool is 30 feet in diameter and 3 feet deep. The second pool measures 6 feet by 12 feet. Both pools are 2 to 3 feet deep and are maintained at around 100° F.

Area attractions: Ladd Marsh, a 3,000-acre wildlife sanctuary adjacent to RV Resort, is a great place to spend a few hours observing dozens of species of water-fowl. There's a mile-long nature trail through the sanctuary.

The Hot Lake RV Resort is on the 95-mile-long, figure-eight Grande Tour from La Grande through Hot Lake and on to Union and Medical Springs. From Medical Springs the driving tour then heads back to Union and north to Cove before returning to La Grande. This is a nice day-long tour if you're staying in La Grande. Pick up a tour map and area highlight descriptions at the La Grande/Union County Visitors and Convention Bureau.

Cove Warm Springs

Contact information:
Cove Warm Springs
907 Water Street
Cove, OR 97824
(541) 586–4890

General description: A natural warm-water swimming pool and picnic area on the edge of a small town in Oregon's Grande Ronde Valley.

Location: Northeast Oregon, 17 miles east of La Grande in the community of Cove.

Development: A concrete swimming pool encloses the natural warm springs. A small picnic area is adjacent to the pool.

Best times to visit: Late May to Memorial Day. The swimming pool is closed other times of the year.

Restrictions: Swimsuits are required in the pool, and a small fee is charged to swim.

Access: Any vehicle can make the trip on the paved roads to Cove. Pools are open seven days a week, 11:00 A.M. to 8:00 P.M., from Memorial Day to Labor Day.

Water temperature: The warm springs and the swimming pool are both 86° F.

Services: There are a few snacks for sale at the pool. Gas, lodging, and more substantial meals are available in La Grande and Union.

Accommodations: There's no place to stay in Cove, but there are some nice overnight options nearby. The Moss Springs Campground is in the Eagle Cap Wilderness east of Cove. (Take French Street in Cove east until it bends into Mill Creek Lane, which soon becomes FR 6220. This road climbs for 8 miles to the

Cove Warm Springs

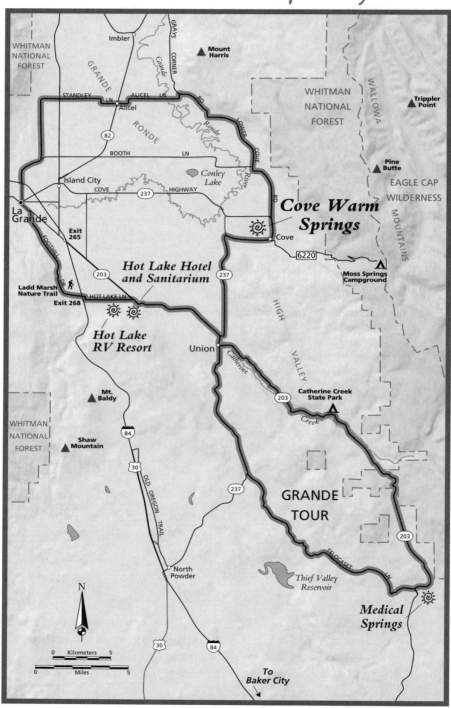

WHITMAN NATIONAL FOREST

Imbler

Mount Harris

GRAY'S CORNER RD.

STANDLEY LN

ALICEL LN

Alicel

82

GRANDE

RONDE

Grande

Ronde

River

BOOTH LN

Island City

COVE

237

HIGHWAY

Conley Lake

LOWER COVE RD

WHITMAN NATIONAL FOREST

WALLOWA MOUNTAINS

Tripler Point

Pine Butte

EAGLE CAP WILDERNESS

Cove Warm Springs

Cove

6220

Moss Springs Campground

La Grande

Exit 265

203

Hot Lake Hotel and Sanitarium

237

HOT LAKE LN

Ladd Marsh Nature Trail

Exit 268

Hot Lake RV Resort

FOOTHILL DR.

Union

Catherine

HIGH VALLEY

203

Catherine Creek State Park

Creek

Mt. Baldy

84

WHITMAN NATIONAL FOREST

Shaw Mountain

30

OLD OREGON TRAIL

237

237

GRANDE TOUR

Thief Valley Reservoir

203

North Powder

TELOCASET LN

Medical Springs

N

Kilometers 0 5

Miles 0 5

84

30

To Baker City

Moss Springs campground.) Another camping location at a lower elevation is Catherine Creek State Park, 8 miles southeast of Union on OR 203. A more upscale option is the Union Hotel, built in 1921 in the American Renaissance style (call 541–562–6135 or visit www.theunionhotel.com).

Map: Oregon State Highway Map.

Finding the springs: From La Grande drive 17 miles east on OR 237 to the town of Cove. Turn left off Main Street onto French Street, and follow the Cove Swimming Pool signs to the pool parking area.

Overview: Although Cove Warm Springs isn't a steaming wilderness soak, it is a nice place for a family swim and picnic on a warm summer afternoon. Unlike many pools where mineral water is piped in, the Cove swimming pool is built directly on top of the warm springs. Most of the pool bottom is concrete, but a 15- by 15-foot opening in the center of the pool exposes bare rock fissures bubbling warm water at more than 300 gallons per minute. The pool doesn't need to be chlorinated, as the large flow rate of the warm springs ensures that the water in the pool turns over several times a day.

Cove Warm Springs swimming pool.

There's a picnic area with big cottonwood trees next to the pool where you can have a late lunch after an hour or two of swimming.

A nearby church camp often sends young people to swim in the pool on hot summer days. According to the pool owner, South Africa's Archbishop Desmond Tutu visited the church camp several years ago and spent an afternoon swimming with the kids in Cove Warm Springs.

Cove Warm Springs has had the same owner for the past three decades. The owner lives in an adjacent house but closes the pool in fall when he heads to Arizona.

Area attractions: The charming Victorian-era town of Union is located about 7 miles south of Cove on OR 237. The Union County Museum features excellent cowboy and geology exhibits, as well as period rooms. The Eagle Cap Wilderness in the Wallowa Mountains east of Cove offers hiking and fishing.

Medical Springs

Contact information: e-mail only—medicalsprings@eoni.com.

General description: A pioneer resort that featured an Olympic-sized swimming pool and large hotel. Now closed to the public.

Location: Northeastern Oregon, 35 miles southeast of La Grande in the foothills of the Wallowa Mountains.

Development: The hot springs have been used commercially since the first bathhouse was built in 1869. The hot water is currently used for heating a private lodge and an Olympic- sized swimming pool.

Best times to visit: OR 203 passes right by Medical Springs, so you can drive through the area any time of the year. You can observe the large swimming pool and old hotel from the road. Unfortunately the pool is off-limits to the public, but it's worth stopping for a quick look.

Water temperature: The hot springs emerge from the ground at 140° F, and then are piped 200 yards to the 50-foot by 150-foot swimming pool, where the water is cooled to around 104° F.

Services: None available at the springs. A small general store at one time operated near the swimming pool, but this has been closed for several years. You'll need to drive to Union or La Grande for gas, groceries, and restaurants.

Accommodations: There's a nice creekside campground in Catherine Creek State Park, 12 miles northwest of Medical Springs on OR 203. A more luxurious lodging option in the nearby town of Union is the Union Hotel, built in 1921 in the American Renaissance style (call 541–562–6135 or visit www.theunionhotel.com).

Map: Oregon State Highway Map.

Medical Springs

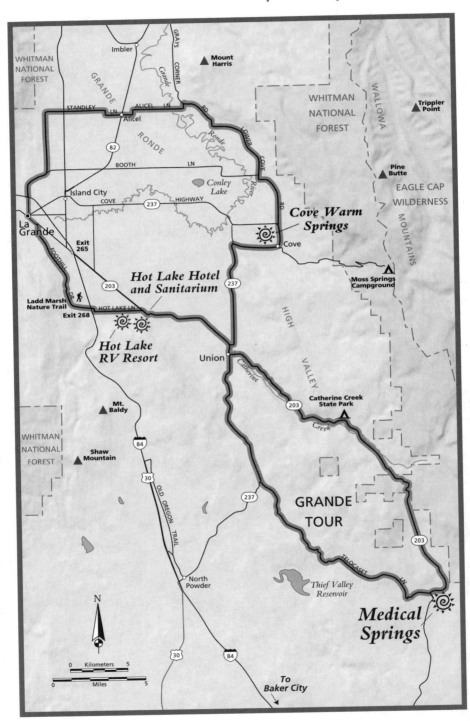

Finding the springs: From La Grande drive 15 miles south on OR 203 to the town of Union. Continue through Union southeast on OR 203 for an additional 20 miles to Medical Springs. Park your car near the general store and walk a few yards south to see the swimming pool.

Overview and History: Medical Springs is inextricably linked to Dunham Wright, one of the most influential frontier politicians in eastern Oregon. Originally from the Midwest, Wright moved to Cove, Oregon, in the early 1860s. Barely twenty years old, Wright was anxious to purchase his own land. A rancher in the area told Wright about some unclaimed property southeast of Cove that had hot springs, and Wright rode out to investigate. Years later, in his memoirs, Wright described his first view of Medical Springs and the Native Americans camped nearby:

> The springs were located in a big willow grove. The men would build a number of small dams across the streams that ran from the springs. The water would accumulate to the depth of about twenty inches. Sticks were placed around the edge, and then a big elk hide or blanket would be stretched across the top to keep the steam in. The men would then crawl in like "dogs in a kennel." When they were done steaming, they would jump into the cold water creek, which they had dammed to about three feet deep. This was thirty yards from the hot springs (where the hotel later stood). The final stage was to get out of the water, wrap themselves in warm blankets, then "lay down to almost melt in their tepees."

Wright's bride, Artemesia, encouraged him to stake a claim to the property, which he did in December of 1868. Wright built a log cabin and a small log bathhouse on the property in 1869. Shortly after moving to Medical Springs, Wright became active in state politics and served for ten years in the Oregon State Legislature.

The little resort attracted visitors from nearby Union and La Grande. In 1886 Wright built his first hotel. The two-story structure measured 26 by 100 feet and contained forty guest rooms. In 1905 he added a sanitarium and additional rooms to the hotel, as well as a livery stable, a general store, and a post office. The remodeled hotel featured two parlors, "one with a pool table for the men, and the other a piano for the women." A large maple-floored ballroom occupied the upper floor.

Visitors to Medical Springs in 1895.   PHOTO: COURTESY OREGON HISTORICAL SOCIETY

Wright was proud of the beautiful surroundings of his resort. A brochure produced to market the resort claimed that "the pure mountain air, the grand scenery, the excellent fishing and hunting are valuable adjuncts in tempting the invalid out of his morbid self, and fostering in him renewed courage and hope."

Unlike the fancy hotel and sanitarium at nearby Hot Lake, which attracted well-heeled visitors, Wright's resort attracted a rough-edged crowd, including "miners with rheumatism, gamblers who played a hard game of cards and smoked old stogies, and rowdy, drunken cowboys over-zealous with their six-shooters." For a time Wright sponsored a rodeo at the resort. Apparently the popular event ended when, according to his grandson, Wright realized that he couldn't control the crowd: "too many drunken cowboys and only one sheriff per county." Even normally genteel activities at the resort were boisterous. One newspaper article noted that "irate croquet players were known to end a match by shooting at the balls."

A fire destroyed the wooden hotel in 1917. Wright had not adequately insured the structure and only had enough funds to build a smaller six-room hotel on the property the following year. In 1929 Wright built the open-air pool that is still used by his descendants. He continued to live at the resort until his death in 1942, shortly after his one-hundredth birthday.

Medical Springs closed to the public in the 1950s, when a lumber mill in a nearby town went out of business. Most of the town residents who had frequented

Medical Springs were thrown out of work and left the area, which caused a drastic reduction in resort revenues.

Wright's great granddaughter resides at Medical Springs, and her son-in-law helps take care of the property. The swimming pool is closed to the public, but Wright's family members swim in the warm waters. The current owners are thinking of reopening the hotel and pool as part of a bed-and-breakfast operation.

Area attractions: The charming Victorian-era town of Union is 20 miles northwest of Medical Springs. Union County Museum has excellent cowboy and geology exhibits, as well as period rooms. The Eagle Cap Wilderness northeast of Medical Springs offers several hiking trails to high mountain lakes.

Consider driving the 95-mile-long circular Grande Tour from La Grande to Hot Lake and on to Union and Medical Springs. The tour then circles back to Union and north to Cove before returning to La Grande. This is a good daylong tour if you're staying in La Grande or Union. In addition to Medical Springs, you'll see the hot springs at Hot Lake and the warm-water swimming pool in Cove. Pick up a tour map and area-highlight descriptions at the La Grande/Union County Visitors and Convention Bureau.

Crystal Crane Hot Springs

Contact information:
Crystal Crane Hot Springs
HC 73–2653 Highway 78
Burns, OR 97720
(541) 493–2312
www.crystalcranehotsprings.com

General description: A small resort with an open-air hot pool and enclosed soaking tubs, situated on windswept sagebrush flats.

Location: Southeast Oregon, about 25 miles southeast of Burns.

Development: Privately owned and developed.

Best times to visit: Autumn, winter, and spring are best for soaking in the indoor soaking tubs. The cooler outdoor pool is a favorite in the summer months. According to the present owners, the resort keeps busy year-round, but they rarely have to turn people away. Hunters, school children from the nearby town of Crane, and tourists heading toward Steens Mountain and the Alvord Desert are the resort's main customers.

Restrictions: The outdoor soaking pool and the indoor soaking tubs are open from 9:00 A.M. to 9:00 P.M. every day. Bathing suits must be worn in the open-air hot springs pond. What you wear in the private enclosed hot tubs is up to you. A fee is charged for soaking and overnight accommodations.

Access: Any vehicle can make the trip along OR 78 to the hot springs.

Water temperature: Hot water is pumped from two wells on the property, one around 180° F and the second a cooler 120° F. Water from a cold-water well is mixed with the hot well water in the soaking pond and hot tubs. The hot-springs pond varies seasonally between 90° and 102° F, whereas the private soaking tubs can be adjusted to any desired soaking temperature.

Crystal Crane Hot Springs

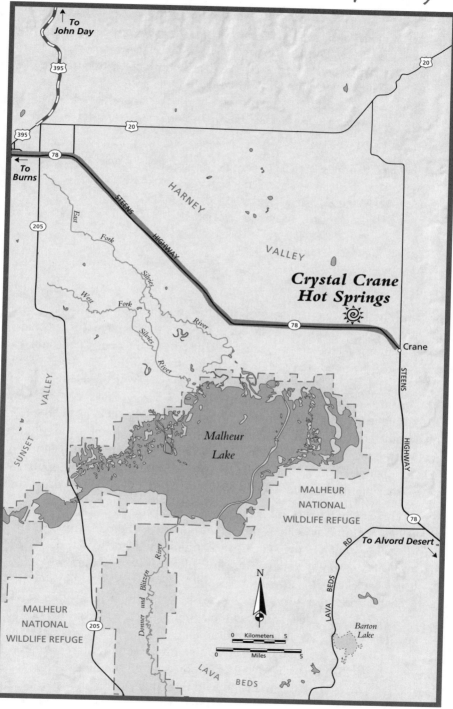

Services: Stop at Crane Supply 3 miles southeast of the hot springs for what are claimed to be the "Best Hamburgers in the County." Stock up either there or in Burns on supplies you'll need if you're staying a few days at the hot springs.

Accommodations: The resort features a dozen camping spots with fire pits and twenty full-service RV spaces. For more comfortable lodging stay in one of the five small cabins or in the recently completed ten-room motel. Visitors traveling with horses can take advantage of a horse corral and exercise area. The current owners are completing a small meeting room next to the motel, which will be the only public-meeting facility available within 30 miles.

Map: Oregon State Highway Map,

Finding the springs: From Burns drive 25.5 miles southeast on OR 78. Look for the Crystal Crane Hot Springs sign on the north side of the highway (between Mileposts 25 and 26). Turn left and drive about 0.1 mile to the hot-springs parking lot. The small town of Crane is located about 3.5 miles southeast of the hot springs.

Overview: The large open-air soaking pond is about 80 feet in diameter, gently graduating in depth from its grassy edges to more than 12 feet in its center. A wooden platform extends a few feet in from the edge of the pool. Picnic tables are available near the pond (bring your own lunches).

The bathhouse adjacent to the soaking pond contains six individual soaking tubs. The tubs are made from galvanized livestock watering tanks, which provides a truly unique soaking experience. The private, wood-paneled tub rooms are rented by the hour, and water temperature can be adjusted as hot as you can stand it. Four of the soaking tubs are oblong (about 3 feet by 10 feet) and can easily hold two to four people. Two larger circular tubs are available for bigger groups or families. All soaking tubs are about 3 feet deep.

History: Three natural hot springs flowed onto the sagebrush prairie for thousands of years before European settlers moved into the surrounding Harney Valley. In the early 1900s women from the nearby community of Crane sometimes did their laundry in the hot springs. They strung their clotheslines near the springs so that the clean, wet clothes could dry in the high desert breezes. One innovative housewife transported a hand-operated washing machine to the hot springs. Local ranchers also took advantage of the commercial benefits of the hot water. The ranchers would drive truckloads of butchered hogs to the property, where they dipped the carcasses into the scalding water to loosen the animal hides.

In the 1920s the hot springs acquired a more sophisticated use. Minne Iland, a local physician, formed a partnership with entrepreneur Ralph Catterson and

Crystal Crane Hot Springs east of Burns, Oregon.

built a 30- by 60-foot swimming pool near the springs, piping the 180° F. artesian hot water into the pool. No cold water was yet available at the little resort, so bathers had to wait a day or more for the water to cool enough to their liking. Iland and Catterson also built a dance hall and a restaurant near the swimming pool. Taking the last initials of their names, Iland and Catterson christened their little resort "I and C Hot Springs." The wooden dance hall and restaurant were destroyed in a fire in the 1930s and were never rebuilt.

From the 1930s until the 1990s, a series of entrepreneurs managed the hot springs. One local named Shorty Lasater opened a gas station and grocery store near the springs in the 1930s, but the business survived only a few years. Now the only remnant of these many commercial ventures is a decaying concrete swimming pool located behind the new motel.

The current renovation of Crystal Crane Hot Springs is due to the hard work of Dan and Denise Kryger, who purchased the property in 1997. The Krygers are responsible for many improvements at the resort, including the hot-tub rooms, motel, cabins, and upgraded RV facilities.

Area attractions: The 183,000-acre Malheur Wildlife Refuge, situated about 25 miles from Crystal Crane Hot Springs (south of Burns on OR 205), is a major resting area for migrating birds on the Pacific Flyway. More than 250 species of birds have been identified on the refuge. Malheur Cave is located 17 miles east of the hot springs. Stretching more than 3,000 feet in length, the cave is really a lava tube, formed thousands of years ago when volcanic lava solidified around a fast-moving river of molten rock. When the interior lava spilled out of the tube, the solid-rock walls of the tube remained, forming the present cave. Another geologist's delight is Diamond Craters, located 25 miles south of the hot springs. Diamond Craters contain an outstanding selection of volcanic formations, including lava tubes and cinder cones.

Mickey Hot Springs

Contact information:
Bureau of Land Management
Burns District Office
HC 74–12533 Highway 20 West
Hines, OR 97738
(541) 573–4400
www.or.blm.gov

General description: A slumbering series of thermal features that during wet years may transform into a display of mud pots, hissing steam vents, and Oregon's only natural geyser.

Location: Southeastern Oregon, 101 miles southeast of Burns in the Alvord Desert.

Development: The hot springs and adjacent dry desert lake-beds are undeveloped, except for the Bureau of Land Management (BLM) fence that encloses the twenty acres surrounding the springs.

Best times to visit: You'll have the best chance of seeing gurgling mud pots, and perhaps even the active geyser, during spring in years when there has been lots of rainfall (which doesn't happen all that often). The thermal activity is much quieter during normal years, when little rain falls (After all, that's why this is a desert!). Try to miss the scorching temperatures of July and August.

Restrictions: The BLM doesn't encourage soaking at Mickey Hot Springs due to the high temperatures and fragile nature of some of the geothermal formations. Signs are posted warning of the scalding temperatures in the thermal pools.

Access: The gravel Fields-Denio Road is accessible by most vehicles. The final 6 miles to the hot springs is a heavily washboarded dirt road. During the rare rainstorms in the Alvord Desert, this road may be too muddy to drive.

Mickey Hot Springs

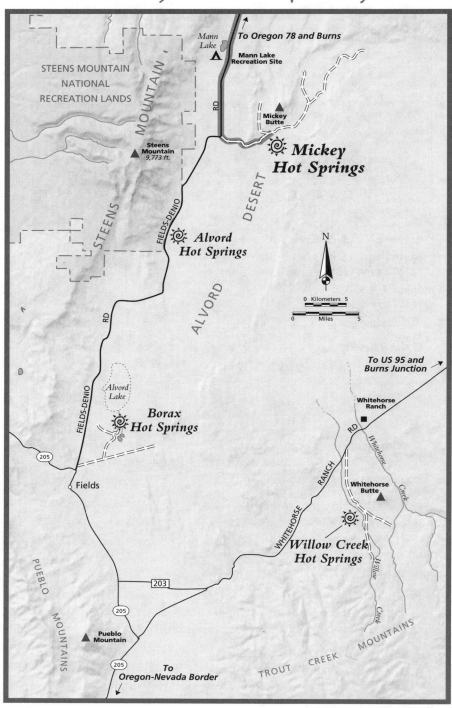

Mann Lake

To Oregon 78 and Burns

Mann Lake Recreation Site

STEENS MOUNTAIN NATIONAL RECREATION LANDS

Mickey Butte

Mickey Hot Springs

Steens Mountain 9,773 ft.

DESERT

Alvord Hot Springs

ALVORD

N

0 Kilometers 5

0 Miles 5

RD

FIELDS-DENIO

Alvord Lake

Borax Hot Springs

To US 95 and Burns Junction

Whitehorse Ranch

RD

Whitehorse Creek

205

Fields

WHITEHORSE RANCH

Whitehorse Butte

Willow Creek Hot Springs

Willow Creek

203

205

PUEBLO MOUNTAINS

Pueblo Mountain

205

To Oregon-Nevada Border

TROUT CREEK MOUNTAINS

Water temperature: BLM researchers have recorded temperatures as high as 206° F. in the thermal pools at Mickey Hot Springs. Temperatures vary from year to year and season to season. The temperature in the large main pool measured 130° F. in the autumn of 2001.

Services: No services are available. Be sure you have plenty of water and a full tank of gas before heading for the hot springs—it's a good hour's drive to the nearest store and gas station in Fields.

Accommodations: Camping isn't allowed within the fenced area enclosing the hot springs, but you can camp in the parking area or on most of the thousands of surrounding acres of BLM land. Camping permits are not required. For more picturesque mountain camping, take one of the side roads that wander into the foothills of Steens Mountain west of Fields-Denio Road, and camp anywhere on BLM land. (Check the BLM map to ensure you are on public property.) Camping is also available at BLM's Mann Lake Recreation Site, 7 miles north on Fields-Denio Road from the turnoff to Mickey Hot Springs. No drinking water is available at Mann Lake, so be sure you have plenty with you. The 276-acre lake is popular with fishermen in search of high-desert cutthroat trout.

If you need a more civilized place to sleep, drive on Fields-Denio Road 34 miles south of the Mickey Hot Springs turnoff, and stay at the small motel in Fields. (Call ahead to see if they have rooms available—541–495–2275).

Map: BLM Burns District South Half.

Finding the springs: From Burns drive 65 miles east on OR 78. Turn south onto the gravel Fields-Denio Road (also called the Fields-Follyfarm Road), and drive 31.3 miles toward Fields. Turn east onto a dirt road just north of a cattle guard. Drive 6.4 miles east, skirting the southern tip of Mickey Butte, until you arrive at the small parking area near a BLM sign that warns of the boiling water in Mickey Hot Springs. Park your car near the sign and walk through the narrow gate. Follow a well-marked path about 200 feet east to the main hot pool at Mickey Hot Springs. Take along a copy of the BLM map of the area—the side roads can be confusing.

Overview: Mickey Hot Springs isn't just one hot spring—it's a group of close to two dozen steam vents, hot pools, mud pots, and occasionally a natural geyser. What thermal features you see depends on the time of year you visit and the amount of precipitation that has fallen recently. During extremely wet years the Mickey Hot Springs area is alive with hissing steam vents and gurgling thermal pools. Some of the steaming vents turn into soupy mud pots, bubbling with opaque minerals. The area is the only known location in Oregon that has a natural geyser, although

The main thermal pool at Mickey Hot Springs.

it is rarely seen. In the late 1980s and early 1990s, the geyser was a churning, bubbling pool of 206° F. water and steam that sporadically erupted about a foot into the air. The geyser was even more spectacular during the wet spring of 1992, erupting 6 to 8 feet in the air every one or two minutes.

Unfortunately the geysers and mud pots are rarely seen. Most of the time the geothermal area is fairly quiet, with only a few bubbles in the main pool and some wisps of steam hissing in rock fissures to indicate thermal activity. The largest pool (called the "Morning Glory" by BLM personnel, after the famous thermal pool in Yellowstone National Park) is 20 feet in diameter and more than 10 feet deep. About 10 yards north of the main pool is what appears to be an extinct geyser cone, which has built up over thousands of years to rise more than 8 feet above the surrounding desert. Overflow from Morning Glory pool forms a small stream that flows through a rock channel to a smaller pool about 10 yards to the south. This second pool is about 4 feet wide, 10 feet long, and 3 feet deep. The pool temperature in the overflow pool is around 120° F. The water from this pool flows through another channel toward the flat desert playas, where it pools in cooler and shallower basins. Some visitors attempt to soak in the hot pools at the southern end of the channels, but these pools can still be too hot for comfort. Use extreme caution if you decide to try soaking at Mickey Hot Springs, and keep in mind that the BLM strongly discourages bathing here due to the fragile nature of the area and the wide temperature fluctuations that occur in the thermal pools.

History: For decades the Alvord Ranch held a BLM lease to graze cattle on rangeland surrounding the hot springs. Every year a few diehard hot-springs enthusiasts would visit the springs and soak in one of the runoff channels from the scalding thermal pools, but for much of the year the hot springs bubbled in solitude. In the early 1990s Mickey Hot Springs caught the attention of the press when the geyser began to erupt regularly to a height of 8 feet or more. More than 2,000 people visited the hot springs that year to see the eruptions.

Concerned with the impact of increasing numbers of visitors, the BLM conducted an environmental assessment on the hot springs in 1995. Two years later the BLM built a fence around the hot springs to keep both cattle and cars from damaging the fragile thermal features. (According to a BLM spokesman, a few calves from the Alvord Ranch that graze on BLM land have fallen into the hot springs over the years.) A zigzag opening in the fence allows visitors to pass through while keeping cattle outside.

A sad chapter occurred in the history of Mickey Hot Springs in the autumn of 1996. A hunter found the dead body of a man in a 117° F. thermal pool. A total eclipse of the moon had been predicted the night before, and police surmised that the man had watched the lunar event while soaking in the solitude of the desert springs. It's unknown how long the man soaked in the hot pool or whether the high water temperature and long soaking time led to a heart attack.

Area attractions: Few visitors make Mickey Hot Springs their sole destination on a trip to the Alvord Desert. Combine your search for Oregon's elusive natural geyser with a trip to Borax Lake and a soak in Alvord Hot Springs, and then head to the cooler high country of Steens Mountain to the west.

Alvord Hot Springs

Contact information:
Bureau of Land Management
Burns District Office
HC 74-12533 Highway 20 West
Hines, OR 97738
(541) 573–4400
www.or.blm.gov

General description: A pair of rustic, concrete soaking pools on the edge of the Alvord Desert.

Location: Southeast Oregon, 107 miles southeast of Burns.

Development: Semideveloped (a small open-air bathhouse was built near the hot springs decades ago). Although not a totally natural soak, the isolated, remote location will bring smiles to the faces to all but the most fanatical hot-springs purists.

Best times to visit: Autumn, winter, and spring are excellent times to soak at Alvord Hot Springs. Visiting during the desert heat of July and August is less appealing. Leave the desert (and the hot springs) to the lizards and wait until cooler fall weather.

Restrictions: No restrictions. Expect nudity in the soaking pools.

Access: The hot springs are privately owned by the Alvord Ranch, but the landowner graciously allows the public to use the hot springs without charge. Please respect the rare generosity of this landowner by treating the hot springs and surrounding property with respect. Any vehicle can make the trip on the graveled Fields-Denio Road to the parking area adjacent to the hot springs. A rare snowstorm may block portions of Fields-Denio Road in the winter.

Alvord Hot Springs

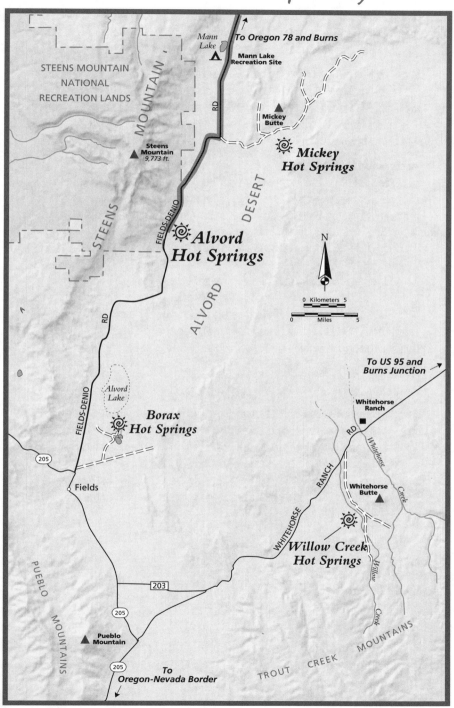

STEENS MOUNTAIN
NATIONAL
RECREATION LANDS

Mann Lake

To Oregon 78 and Burns

Mann Lake
Recreation Site

Mickey
Butte

Mickey
Hot Springs

Steens
Mountain
9,773 ft.

ALVORD DESERT

*Alvord
Hot Springs*

ALVORD

STEENS

FIELDS-DENIO

RD

N

0 Kilometers 5

0 Miles 5

To US 95 and
Burns Junction

Whitehorse
Ranch

Alvord
Lake

*Borax
Hot Springs*

FIELDS-DENIO

RD

Whitehorse
Butte

Whitehorse Creek

205

Fields

WHITEHORSE RANCH RD

*Willow Creek
Hot Springs*

Willow Creek

PUEBLO

203

205

MOUNTAINS

Pueblo
Mountain

205

To
Oregon-Nevada Border

TROUT CREEK MOUNTAINS

Water temperature: The hot springs emerge along a series of 170° F. seeps on the east side of Fields-Denio Road. Hot water then meanders 100 yards east, cooling to about 120° F. by the time it reaches the two soaking pools. The actual soaking temperature usually varies between 100° and 115° F, depending on how rapidly the hot-springs water is piped into the pools.

Services: None available at the hot springs. The tiny town of Fields (population fourteen) is located 23 miles to the south, where food, gas, and drinking water are available. The Fields Café serves huge breakfasts, hamburger lunches, and dinner. The cafe is famous for its thick milkshakes—check the chart on the restaurant wall to see how many shakes have been sold since January 1.

Accommodations: Camping isn't allowed at the privately owned hot springs, but plenty of options abound on nearby BLM land. Take one of the side roads that wander into the foothills of Steens Mountain west of the hot springs, and camp anywhere on BLM land. (Check the BLM map to ensure you are on public property before rolling out your sleeping bag for the night.) Camping permits are not required. Camping is also available at BLM's Mann Lake Recreation Site, 18 miles north of Alvord Hot Springs on Fields-Denio Road. No drinking water is available at Mann Lake, so be sure you have plenty with you. Four BLM campgrounds are also available on Steens Loop Road on the west side of Steens Mountain. If you need a more civilized place to lay your head, drive 23 miles south of the hot springs and stay at the small motel in Fields. (Call ahead to see if they have rooms available—541–495–2275.)

Map: BLM Burns District South Half.

Finding the springs: From Burns drive 65 miles east on OR 78. Turn south onto the gravel Fields-Denio Road (also called the Fields-Follyfarm Road), and drive 42 miles toward Fields. You'll see the steaming hot springs and tin-sided bathhouse about 100 yards east of the road. Park on the side of the road near a cattleguard, and walk on the well-trod path east to the soaking pools.

If you've been visiting Mickey Hot Springs to the north, Alvord Hot Springs is 10.5 miles south on Fields-Denio Road from the intersection with the turnoff to Mickey Hot Springs.

Overview: The pools at Alvord Hot Springs have hosted decades of local ranchers, bird and elk hunters, and tourists enjoying the Steens Mountain and Alvord Desert area. The two adjoining soaking pools are each about 8 feet square and 4 feet deep. Corrugated tin sheeting surrounds the northernmost pool. Judging from the numerous bullet holes visible in the metal walls, this pool has seen more

Alvord Hot Springs with Steens Mountain in the distance.

than a few wild parties. There's no roof over either pool, which allows great views of the stars at night. A small bench sits on the wooden deck on the east side of the enclosed pool. South of the enclosed pool is the open-air pool, which tends to be the more popular of the two because of its unobstructed views of Steens Mountain and the dry desert lake beds. Old ceramic washtubs have been placed upside down in the pools to provide quirky but comfortable seating for bathers.

Alvord Hot Springs has a unique temperature-control system. Two-inch steel pipes divert the 120° F. water from the hot creek to the lip of the soaking pools. The pipes quickly fill the soaking pools to an uncomfortably hot temperature if the hot water flow is left unchecked. Fortunately the ends of the hot-water pipes can be raised about a foot into the air and placed on a concrete block, which allows gravity to stop the flow of hot water. Once the hot water flow is stopped, the pools will eventually cool to a comfortable bathing temperature.

There's also a wooden stopper in the bottom of each pool, which can be removed to allow the water to drain completely before filling for a fresh soak.

You never know what the water temperature will be in the Alvord Hot Springs pools when you first arrive, as it depends on whether the previous bathers had left the hot water flowing into the pool or had diverted the flow to cool things down. Either way it usually only takes a half hour or so to adjust the hot-water flow to reach a comfortable soaking temperature.

The runoff from Alvord Hot Springs provides moisture for one of the few bird habitats in the Alvord Desert. Long-billed curlews nest in this area, and American avocets, snowy plovers, and killdeers can be found farther east on the playa.

Area attractions: The 30-mile-long Steens Mountain towers more than 5,000 feet above the Alvord Desert. Steens Mountain Loop Road, a scenic 52-mile traverse from the lower foothills to the mountain summit, starts 8 miles south of Frenchglen (northwest of Fields). East of Alvord Hot Springs stretch the usually dry desert lake beds (or "playas"). The massive ridge of Steens Mountain to the west creates a rain shadow farther east, creating the harsh, dry environment of the Alvord Desert. During occasional wet years the lake beds may contain a shallow layer of water for a couple of months, but for most of the year the playas are dry and dusty. Plan on spending a couple of days exploring other geothermal springs in the Alvord Desert, including Borax Lake, Mickey Hot Springs, and Willow Creek Hot Springs.

Borax Lake and Borax Hot Springs

Contact information:
The Nature Conservancy of Oregon
821 Southeast Fourteenth Avenue
Portland, Oregon 97214
(503) 230–1221
Fax: 503-230-9639
nature.org/wherewework/northamerica/states/oregon/preserves/art6794.html

Bureau of Land Management
Burns District
HC 74-12533, Highway 20 West
Hines, OR 97738
(541) 573–4400
www.or.blm.gov

General description: A string of more than a dozen hot springs that march north along a fault line in the Oregon desert. The thermal water from the southernmost hot springs creates a five-acre warm-water lake.

Location: Southeast Oregon, 7.5 miles north of Fields in the Alvord Desert.

Development: Undeveloped. The ruins of an old steel vat used to refine borax lie next to Borax Lake.

Best times to visit: Floating in the lukewarm waters of Borax Lake is best done during mild, dry days in late spring and early summer and again in autumn. Wading through the shallow water on the edge of Borax Lake to the lake's

Borax Lake and Borax Hot Springs

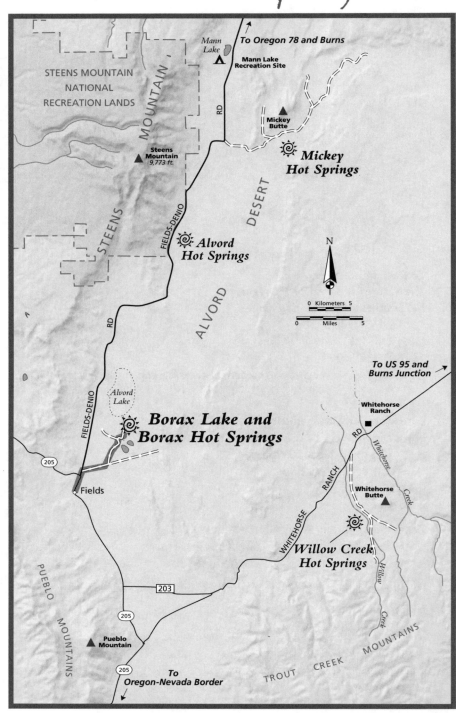

STEENS MOUNTAIN
NATIONAL
RECREATION LANDS

Mann Lake

To Oregon 78 and Burns

Mann Lake Recreation Site

STEENS MOUNTAIN, MOUNTAIN

Mickey Butte

Mickey Hot Springs

Steens Mountain 9,773 ft.

FIELDS-DENIO RD

DESERT

Alvord Hot Springs

N

ALVORD

0 Kilometers 5

0 Miles 5

To US 95 and Burns Junction

Whitehorse Ranch

Alvord Lake

FIELDS-DENIO RD

Borax Lake and Borax Hot Springs

WHITEHORSE RANCH RD

Whitehorse Creek

205

Fields

Whitehorse Butte

Willow Creek Hot Springs

Willow Creek

203

PUEBLO MOUNTAINS

205

Pueblo Mountain

TROUT CREEK MOUNTAINS

205

To Oregon-Nevada Border

deeper and warmer center can be a chilly proposition in winter. Driving on the dirt roads in the area could be difficult after one of the rare rainstorms in spring. Avoid the searing summer heat of July and August.

Restrictions: No restrictions, but use extreme caution around the scalding hot springs, some of which approach 180° F. Signs posted by the BLM warn visitors that they could break through the thin crust surrounding some of these hot springs, so avoid standing too close to the edge of the hot pools.

Access: High-clearance vehicles are recommended on the bumpy dirt access road, but if you take your time, almost any vehicle can make the trip.

Water temperature: The five-acre Borax Lake ranges from 84° F. near its shallow shore to 95° F. in the deep center of the lake. The source of the lake's warmth is a hot spring that is perhaps hundreds of feet deep in the center of the lake. This geothermal resource is rumored to pump more than 1,000 gallons per minute of 200° F. water into the lake bottom. Don't worry about getting poached in Borax Lake, as the deep hot-spring water cools to a comfortable bathing temperature by the time it rises to the lake's surface.

The series of hot springs north of Borax Lake vary in temperature from 90° F. to more than 170° F. It's hard to tell just by looking at these springs which ones are safe for soaking or whether they are dangerously hot.

Services: No services are available at Borax Lake or Borax Hot Springs. The tiny town of Fields (population fourteen) is located 7.5 miles to the south, where a restaurant, gas, and drinking water are available.

Accommodations: Camping isn't allowed at the lake or the hot springs, but plenty of options abound on nearby BLM land, where camping permits are not required. Take one of the side roads that wander into the foothills of Steens Mountain northwest of Borax Lake and camp anywhere on BLM land. (Check the BLM map to ensure you are on public property before rolling out your sleeping bag for the night.) Camping is also available at BLM's Mann Lake Recreation Site, 31 miles north of Fields on Fields-Denio Road. (No drinking water is available at Mann Lake, so be sure you have plenty with you.) Four BLM campgrounds are also available on Steens Loop Road on the west side of Steens Mountain. If you need a more civilized place to lay your head, stay at the small motel in Fields. (Call ahead to see if they have rooms available—541–495–2275.)

Map: BLM Burns District South Half.

Finding the springs: From Fields drive north 1.2 miles to the intersection of OR 205 and Fields-Denio Road. Proceed 0.5 miles north of this intersection on Fields-Denio Road, and then turn east onto a dirt road next to an electrical substation. Head northeast on this dirt road for 2.1 miles, parallel to the overhead power-lines. Turn north on a washboarded road for 2 miles. You'll reach a closed gate with a BLM sign warning about the danger of the scalding water of the hot springs. Go through the gate (close it behind you), and drive another 1 mile on a bumpy dirt road that takes you past Lower Borax Lake, which is too cold for swimming. Continue past Lower Borax Lake for another 0.5 mile until you see the rusting ruins of the steel vat from the borax-processing operation of a century ago. Borax Lake is less than 100 yards east of these ruins. If you want to swim in the warm waters of Borax Lake, park your car along the dirt road that circles the lake and wade through the shallow water until you reach the deep, warm center of the lake.

To reach the series of thermal pools collectively named Borax Hot Springs, continue on the dirt road northwest of Borax Lake. About 0.1 mile north on this road, you'll start to see a string of hot springs about 10 feet east of the road that stretch for half a mile along a fault line running north across the desert. After passing the first four or five hot springs, this road makes a sharp jog to the west to pass through a gate, then jigs back east and then north parallel to another series of six or seven steaming pools. You'll need to backtrack south on this road past Borax Lake to return to the highway, because the dirt road headed north eventually reaches private land protected by a locked gate.

Overview: Borax Lake and the nearby string of hot springs are one of the most unusual geothermal areas in Oregon. The hot pools march single file along an imaginary line that follows a geologic fault beneath the desert's surface.

The five-acre Borax Lake looks nondescript from the shore, but an aerial photo would tell a much more interesting story. The lake is actually the outflow from a hot spring located deep beneath the lake's center. For a truly mystical experience, wade from the lake's edge through the knee-deep water for 50 yards toward the middle of the lake. The lake bed will disappear beneath your feet, and you'll find yourself floating effortlessly in 95° F. water over the warm, dark core of a hot spring that's perhaps hundreds of feet deep.

After you've explored Borax Lake and the nearby ruins of the old borax works, drive or hike along the road north of the lake to see the row of steaming hot springs. Many of these pools approach 170° F. or more, so stay away from the pool edges as you head north on the road. The northernmost pool on this road is sometimes used for soaking. It's located about 0.6 mile from Borax Lake, at the end of the string of hot springs where the road turns west away from the pools. From where the road bends west, walk 10 yards east to see the two large pools connected by a 3-foot-wide land bridge with a footpath over it. The smaller southern pool is about 20 feet by 30 feet and varies from 3 feet to more than 12 feet deep. The pool temperature is around 104° F. The larger pool north of the land bridge, which is approximately 30 by 70 feet, appears to be much deeper than the southern pool.

Thermal pools north of Borax Lake.

The larger pool may be too hot for soaking, as it may exceed 110° F.

A few additional cautionary words if you choose to soak in Borax Lake or the nearby hot springs. The BLM has measured arsenic levels in the lake and hot springs more than twenty-five times higher than acceptable drinking standards, so if you soak, don't imbibe. If you decide to soak in the northernmost hot springs pool past Borax Lake, remember that the water temperature in these pools can vary drastically from the pool's surface to its depth. Also the fragile crusts surrounding these hot springs may collapse under your weight, so walk with care.

It may be best to confine your soaks to Borax Lake, which seems to have the most stable temperature. But even in the lake, you may feel guilty about splashing around in the only home of the endangered Borax Lake chub, not to mention concerns about the high arsenic levels in the water. Like many visitors you may decide to simply enjoy observing this amazing concentration of geothermal activity and save your soaking for nearby Alvord Hot Springs.

History: In 1897 Charles Taylor heard rumors of extensive deposits of alkali in the southern Alvord Desert. Taylor operated a small borax mine in Nevada and was interested in finding other borax deposits that he could develop. Taylor traveled across the Nevada/Oregon border and discovered large deposits of snow-white sodium borate surrounding Borax Lake. A rancher named Robert Doan owned the mineral-encrusted property, which he considered useless for ranching. It

Borax Lake.

didn't take much convincing for Doan to accept Taylor's offer of $7,000 for the 3,000 acres of the "worthless" land surrounding Borax Lake.

By 1898 Taylor and his partner, John M. Fulton, had moved their borax operation from Nevada to Borax Lake. Fulton hired a chemist named Christian Ollgard to devise a unique method for processing the raw sodium borate into the refined crystalline form needed by customers on the West Coast. Key to the processing operation were two steel boiling vats that Ollgard built next to Borax Lake. The round-bottomed vats could each hold 6,000 gallons of borate solution. Chinese laborers were hired to fill the vats with raw sodium borate gathered from the desert surface. Ollgard then piped in 97° F. water from the warm center of Borax Lake into the vats to cover the borate minerals. Sulphuric acid was added to the solution as a precipitating agent. Sagebrush was then gathered and burned under the vats for several hours until the solution was heated to boiling. The solution was then allowed to cool, which caused the raw borate to form pure crystalline borax. The snow-white borax crystals were bagged in ninety-pound sacks and then hauled in wagons by up to two dozen mules 150 miles south to Winnemucca, Nevada. More than 55,000 pounds of borax were hauled to Nevada every week.

Taylor and Fulton named their borax operation the "Twenty Mule Team Borax Company," after the hauling method they devised to carry the borax to Nevada. Unfortunately they failed to legally register this name, and within a year a competing borax company in California had taken claim to the now-legendary brand. Taylor and Fulton were forced to change their company name to "Rose Valley Borax Company," a prettier but less memorable moniker.

Taylor and Fulton sold their borax operation to Christian Ollgard in 1902, but by 1907 the declining quality of borate deposits from the surrounding desert led to the closure of the facility. At present only the rusting steel boiling vat and a nearby sod house remind visitors of the bustling borax operation and the twenty-mule-team wagons that once passed through the valley.

For several decades after the Rose Valley Borax Company ceased operation, Borax Lake and the nearby hot springs received little attention and few visitors. All that changed in 1980, when an endangered fish was discovered living in the lake's warm brackish waters. The new species of fish was named the Borax Lake chub (*Gila boraxobius*). Only a few thousand of this half-inch-long fish survive on the edge of Borax Lake, where the temperature remains a constant 85° F. Shortly after the chub's discovery in 1980, the U.S. Fish and Wildlife Service declared the Borax Lake chub an endangered species. The species has not been found anywhere else in the world.

The geothermal-energy potential of the area around Borax Lake also attracted attention. In 1990 the BLM gave permission to a California energy company to drill a geothermal test well near Borax Lake. The energy company hoped to find superheated water that could be used in a turbine to generate electricity. Environmentalists expressed concern that drilling near Borax Lake might disrupt the natural hot springs feeding the lake and change the delicate aquatic environment needed to support the endangered Borax Lake chub. In response to the environmental threats to the endangered fish, the Nature Conservancy obtained a lease to manage Borax Lake and 320 acres of adjoining public land. The test wells were never drilled, but energy companies still remain interested in drilling near the area for high-temperature steam that could power generating plants.

Area attractions: The fossil beds located in the Trout Creek area southeast of Fields are worth an afternoon visit. If you're lucky, you may find a beautiful jet-black fossil of prehistoric fern, which stands in stark contrast to the surrounding snow-white rock strata. Stop at the cafe in Fields for directions to the fossil beds.

If you have a few days available to explore the area, consider hiking one of the rarely visited gems of the Oregon State Parks trail system—the 100-mile-long Desert Hiking Trail. The trail starts at the Nevada border south of Fields and heads northwest to the top of Steens Mountain.

33

Willow Creek (Whitehorse Ranch) Hot Springs

Contact information:
Bureau of Land Management
Burns District Office
HC 74-12533 Highway 20 West
Hines, OR 97738
(541) 573–4400
www.or.blm.gov

General description: One of Oregon's most remote rustic soaking pools, surrounded by sagebrush and low mountain ridges.

Location: Southeastern Oregon, 140 miles southeast of Burns.

Development: The hot springs are part of a BLM campground and recreation area, but development is limited to a few fire pits and a well-built privy. The area surrounding the natural hot springs has been enlarged and deepened, and a small concrete-and-rock dam separates the smaller, hot soaking pool from the larger, cooler pool.

Best times to visit: May to October are prime times for visiting, although the hot springs are open year-round. Try to avoid the searing hot weather in midsummer, as well as times when the roads turn to muck due to heavy rains. The campground is often filled with hunters in late fall during hunting season.

Restrictions: Camping isn't allowed within 100 feet of the hot springs. The BLM has imposed a fourteen-day limit to camping at the hot springs and elsewhere on land in the BLM Burns District. Nudity is common in the hot springs pools.

Willow Creek (Whitehorse Ranch) Hot Springs

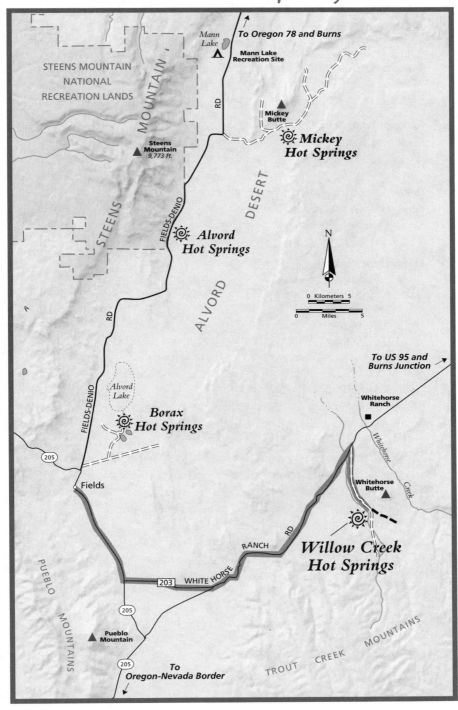

STEENS MOUNTAIN
NATIONAL
RECREATION LANDS

Mann
Lake

To Oregon 78 and Burns

Mann Lake
Recreation Site

Mickey
Butte

*Mickey
Hot Springs*

Steens
Mountain
9,773 ft.

*Alvord
Hot Springs*

N

0 Kilometers 5

0   Miles   5

**To US 95 and
Burns Junction**

Whitehorse
Ranch

Alvord
Lake

*Borax
Hot Springs*

Whitehorse
Butte

205

Fields

*Willow Creek
Hot Springs*

RANCH

203 WHITE HORSE

Whitehorse Creek

PUEBLO

MOUNTAINS

205

Pueblo
Mountain

205

**To
Oregon-Nevada Border**

TROUT CREEK MOUNTAINS

Access: Just about any vehicle can make the trip during dry weather. The last couple of miles to the hot springs can become impassable during rainy weather, when the normally dry and dusty road is transformed into deep slippery mud.

Water temperature: The soaking pool containing the hot springs averages 102° F., whereas the overflow pool varies between 85° and 95° F.

Services: None at the hot springs. Because it's more than an hour's drive to the nearest store, be sure to have a full tank of gas and plenty of food and water before starting your trip.

Accommodations: Camping accommodations only. Willow Creek Hot Springs is a BLM recreation site; camping areas with fire pits are located within a few hundred yards of the hot springs. Camping spots are first-come first-served, and camping permits are not required. If others are camped near the fire pits and you desire more privacy (and a more natural setting), take your sleeping gear a few hundred yards south and find a secluded spot near the shrub-lined banks of aptly named Willow Creek. Dispersed camping is also allowed in the surrounding Wilderness Study Areas and other nearby BLM lands; permits are not required.

Map: BLM Burns District South Half.

Finding the springs: Visitors to Willow Creek Hot Springs often first loop south through the Alvord Desert for a day or two, visiting Alvord Hot Springs, Mickey Hot Springs, and Borax Lake. If you are already in the Alvord Desert, start your drive to Willow Creek Hot Springs at the tiny town of Fields (stock up at the local store with drinking water and gas). From Fields drive south on OR 205 toward the Nevada border for 8.2 miles to CR 203 (the Whitehorse Ranch Road). Drive east on CR 203 for 25 miles (the road turns northeast about 10 miles into this drive). After driving 25 miles on CR 203, look for a poorly marked dirt road on the right (south). You'll spot a telephone pole marked #292 near the turnoff to the dirt road. Take the turnoff and drive south. You'll soon see a bullet-ridden BLM sign that says IMPASSABLE IN WET WEATHER. Believe the sign—dirt roads in this area turn into sticky gumbo after rainstorms. Drive a total of 2.3 miles south on the dirt road until you see a rocky rise on the right with a concrete outhouse at its base. Take the right fork on the dirt road toward the outhouse, passing the hot springs pool as you enter the campground.

The trickiest part of this drive is finding the turnoff to the dirt road from CR 203. Locals use the Whitehorse Ranch headquarters as their main point of reference, so if you overshoot the dirt road, keep going another 2 or 3 miles on CR 203 to the main gate of the Whitehorse Ranch. You can then turn around and reset your odometer, then drive 2.7 miles back southwest on CR 203 and look for telephone pole #292 and the dirt road that leads to Willow Creek Hot Springs.

You can also drive south to Willow Creek Hot Springs from Burns Junction, about 91 miles southeast of Burns on OR 78. From Burns Junction head south on US 95 for 21 miles to the Whitehorse Ranch Road intersection (CR 203). Drive southwest for 21 miles on CR 203 to the Whitehorse Ranch headquarters. Continue southwest past the ranch headquarters for 2.7 miles until you see a dirt road on the left (south), near telephone pole #292. Take this dirt road south for 2.5 miles to Willow Creek Hot Springs.

Overview: Willow Creek Hot Springs is perfect for persons seeking a truly isolated soak far from population centers. The hot springs pool measures about 10 feet by 50 feet, but is divided into two pools by a low concrete dam. The smaller soaking pool averages 102° to 104° F. Stone steps lead down the side of the smaller hot pool, which is about 3 feet deep. Try feeling around with your toes in the mud and gravel center of this pool to find the 110° F. hot spots that are the source of the hot water. Water from the smaller pool flows over the low dam into the larger pool. The temperature in the larger pool averages between 85° and 95° F. Start your soaking experience in the hotter pool and then slip over the dam into the larger pool to cool down.

It's almost imperative that you stay overnight at Willow Creek Hot Springs, given the long driving distances needed to reach this spot. Plan on arriving by midafternoon and setting up your camp and then soak in the hot springs while watching the sun drop down beyond the sagebrush plains.

History: Camp C. F. Smith was the first significant development in the area, built as an army post along the Oregon Central Military Road in 1866. When the army abandoned the post in 1869, a Virginian named John Devine acquired the buildings and converted them and the surrounding land into a major ranching operation. Devine was said to be a dashing figure who often surveyed his ranch properties from the back of a beautiful white horse, which led to the naming of the Whitehorse Ranch (Willow Creek Hot Springs is better known to many locals as Whitehorse Hot Springs). Besides his ranching interests Devine was devoted to raising racehorses, and in 1879 he built an impressive horse barn near the present entrance to the Whitehorse Ranch headquarters. A large, wooden white horse sits atop the horse barn, which still serves as a major landmark in the isolated ranching country of southeastern Oregon. The Whitehorse Ranch is currently one of Oregon's largest ranches, encompassing more than 68,000 acres.

Area attractions: The hot springs are sandwiched between the Trout Creek and Oregon Canyon Mountains, and seven Wilderness Study Areas lie within 15 miles of Willow Creek. Backpacking along the low mountain ridges and vegetated canyons is a popular activity. Hunters use the hot springs as a staging area for mule-deer and sage-grouse hunts. Fishing is allowed in some area streams, although Willow Creek, which flows by the hot springs, is off-limits to anglers. A

Scenic soaking pools at Willow Creek Hot Springs.

rare inland species of cutthroat trout (the Lahontan cutthroat) is the only fish found in Willow Creek and is listed as a federally threatened species. Take a walk along Willow Creek and see if you can spot this rare fish, but leave your fishing pole in your car.

Bibliography

Belknap Resort & Hot Springs—An Historical Guide 1854–1996. McKenzie Bridge, Oreg.: 1996.

Berry, George. "Thermal Springs List for the United States." NOAA Key to Geophysical Records Documentation No. 12. Boulder, Colo.: National Geophysical and Solar-Terrestrial Data Center, 1980.

Blinn, Mayme Schwartz and Richard Joseph. *Upper John Day River—Early Days in Prairie City*. Prairie City, Oreg.: privately printed, 1977.

Bloomquist, Elsie. "A History of Carson." *Skamania County Heritage* 14, no.1 (June, 1985).

Bloomquist, R. Gordon. *Geothermal Energy in Washington: Site Data Base and Development Status*. Klamath Falls, Oreg.: OIT Geo-Heat Utilization Center, 1979.

Fiege, Bennye. *The Story of Soap Lake*. Soap Lake, Wash.: Soap Lake Chamber of Commerce, n.d.

Foster, Teressa. *Settlers in Summer Lake*. Bend, Oreg.: Maverick Publications, 1989.

Hill, Lawrence D. *Tales from the Hills*. Ontario, Oreg.: Daily Argus Observer, 1982.

Horowitz, Howard. "The Landscapes of Hot Springs and Mineral Springs in Western Oregon." Master's thesis, University of Oregon, 1973.

Irving, Washington. *Astoria, or Anecdotes of an Enterprise Beyond the Rocky Mountains*. Philadelphia, Pa.: Carey, Lea, & Blanchard, 1836.

Jackson, Royal G., and Jennifer A. Lee. *Harney County—An Historical Inventory*. Burns, Oreg.: Harney County Historical Society, 1978.

Jensen, Veryl M. *Early Days on the Upper Willamette*. Oakridge, Oreg.: Upper Willamette Pioneer Association, 1970.

Justus, Debra. *Geothermal Resources in Oregon: Site Data Base and Development Status*. Klamath Falls, Oreg.: OIT Geo-Heat Utilization Center, 1979.

Korosec, M.A., et al. *Geothermal Resources of Washington—Geologic Map GM-25*. Olympia, Wash.: Washington Department of Natural Resources, 1981.

Peters, Shirley, and Sheila Smith. *Hot Lake—The Town Under One Roof*. La Grande, Oreg.: privately printed, 1997.

Peterson, Norman V., et al. *Geothermal Resources of Oregon* [map]. Portland, Oreg.: Oregon Department of Geology and Mineral Industries, 1982.

Searcey, Mildred. *Way Back When*. Pendleton, Oreg.: East Oregonian Publishing Company, 1972.

Shaffer, Leslie L.D., and Richard Baxter. "Oregon Borax: Twenty Mule Team—Rose Valley History." *Oregon Historical Quarterly* 73, no. 3 (September 1972).

Simerville, Clara L., ed. *One Century of Life: Dunham Wright of Oregon 1842–1942*. Corvallis, Oreg.: privately printed, 1986.

Southworth, Jo. "The Ritter Hot Springs." *Blue Mountain Eagle* (John Day, Oreg.), 23 November 1972.

U.S. Fish and Wildlife Service. *Recovery Plan for the Borax Lake Chub, Gila boraxobius*. Portland, Oreg.: U.S. Fish and Wildlife Service, 1987.

Contact Information

Washington

Olympic Peninsula

Sol Duc Hot Springs Resort
P.O. Box 2169
Port Angeles, WA 98362-0283
(360) 327–3583
fax: (360) 327–3593
www.northolympic.com/solduc

Olympic Hot Springs
Olympic National Park
Wilderness Information Center
3002 Mt. Angeles Road
Port Angeles, WA 98362
(360) 452–0300
Current trail conditions to Olympic Hot
Springs: www.nps.gov/olym/wic/
trailrpt.htm#OLYMPIC

San Juan Islands

Doe Bay Resort and Retreat
P.O. Box 437
Olga, WA 98279
(360) 376–2291
fax: (360) 376–5809
www.doebay.com

Washington State Ferries
Colman Dock/Pier 52
801 Alaskan Way
Seattle WA 98104
(206) 464–6400
www.wsdot.wa.gov/ferries/current
*(Check this Web site for ferry schedules
to/from Orcas Island/Doe Bay Resort.)*

Washington Cascades

Baker Hot Spring
Mount Baker–Snoqualmie National Forest
Baker Ranger District
810 State Route 20
Sedro-Woolley, WA 98284
(360) 856–5700
www.fs.fed.us/r6/mbs

Baker Lake Resort
46110 East Main Street
Concrete, WA 98237
(888) 711–3033

Carson Mineral Hot Springs Resort
P.O. Box 1169
Carson, WA 98610
(509) 427–8292

Friends of Scenic Hot Springs
P.O. Box 268
Skykomish, WA 98288
friendsoshs@hotmail.com

Goldmyer Hot Springs
202 North 85th, #106,
Seattle, WA 98103
(206) 789–5631
www.goldmyer.org

Kennedy Hot Springs
Darrington Ranger District
1405 Emmens Street
Darrington, WA 98241
(360) 436–1155

Scenic Hot Springs
Skykomish Ranger District
74920 Northeast Stevens Pass Highway
P.O. Box 305
Skykomish, WA 98288
(360) 677–2414

Central Washington

Inn at Soap Lake
226 Main Avenue East
Soap Lake, WA 98851–0098
(509) 246–1132
www.innsoaplake.com

Notaras Lodge
13 Canna Street
Soap Lake, Washington 98851
(509) 246–0462
www.notaraslodge.com

Soap Lake Chamber of Commerce
P.O. Box 433
Soap Lake, WA 98851
(509) 246–1821
www.soaplakecoc.org

Soap Lake Conservancy
P.O. Box 65
Soap Lake, WA 98851
(509) 766–1699
www.thelake.org

Oregon

Oregon Cascades

Bagby Hot Springs
Clackamas River Ranger District
595 Northwest Industrial Way
Estacada, OR 97023
(503) 630–6861
www.bagbyhotsprings.org

Belknap Hot Springs Resort
59296 Belknap Springs Road
P.O. Box 2001
McKenzie Bridge, OR 97413
(541) 822–3512

Breitenbush Hot Springs Retreat and
Conference Center
P.O. Box 578
Detroit, OR 97342
(503) 854–3314
www.breitenbush.com

Deer Creek (Bigelow) Hot Springs
McKenzie Ranger District
57600 McKenzie Highway
McKenzie Bridge, OR 97413
(541) 822–3317

Lithia Springs Inn
2165 West Jackson Road
Ashland, OR 97520
(800) 482–7128
www.lithiaspringsinn.com/

McCredie Hot Springs
Middle Fork Ranger District
46375 Highway 58
Westfir, OR 97492
(541) 782–2283

Terwilliger (Cougar) Hot Springs
Blue River Ranger District
57600 Blue River Drive
P.O. Box 199
Blue River, OR 97413
(541) 822–3317
*(Also visit the Friends of Cougar Hot
Springs Web site*: www.cougar.org)

Umpqua Hot Springs
Diamond Lake Ranger District
2020 Toketee Ranger Station Road
Idleyld Park, OR 97447
(541) 498–2531

Wall Creek Hot Springs (Meditation Pool)
Middle Fork Ranger District
46375 Highway 58
Westfir, OR 97492
(541) 782–2283

WellSprings (Jackson Hot Springs)
2253 Highway 99 North
Ashland, OR 97520
(808) 482–3776
wellspringsnet.com

Central Oregon

Antelope Hot Springs
Hart Mountain National Antelope Refuge
Fish and Wildlife Service
National Wildlife Refuge System
18 South G Street
P.O. Box 111
Lakeview, OR 97630-0107
(541) 947–3315
www.recreation.gov/detail.cfm?ID=(1421)

Geyser (Hunter's) Hot Springs Resort
Highway 395 North
Lakeview, OR 97630
(541) 947–4142 or (877) 686–9889

Kah-Nee-Ta Resort
P.O. Box K
Warm Springs, OR 97761
(541) 553–1112 or (800) 554–4SUN (4786)
www.kah-nee-taresort.com

Lakeview Ranger District
HC 64 Box 60
Lakeview, OR 97630
(541) 947–3334
www.fs.fed.us/r6/fremont

Summer Lake Hot Springs
28513 Highway 31
Paisley, OR 97636
(541) 943–3931 or (877) 492–8554
www.summerlakehotsprings.com

Northeast Oregon

Blue Mountain Hot Springs
Star Route
Prairie City, OR 97876
(541) 820–3744

Cove Warm Springs
907 Water Street
Cove, OR 97824
(541) 586–4890

Hot Lake RV Resort
65182 Hot Lake Lane
La Grande, OR 97850
(541) 963–5253 or (800) 994–5253

La Grande/Union County
Visitors & Convention Bureau
1912 Fourth Street, #200
La Grande, OR 97850
(541) 963–8588 or (800) 848–9969
www.visitlagrande.com

Lehman Hot Springs
P.O. Box 187
Ukiah, OR 97880
(541) 427–3015
www.lehmanhotsprings.com

Malheur National Forest
Prairie City Ranger District
P.O. Box 337
Prairie City, OR 97869
(541) 820–3800

Medical Springs
medicalsprings@eoni.com

Ritter Hot Springs
Box 16
Ritter, OR 97872
(541) 421–3846

Southeast Oregon

Alvord Hot Springs
Bureau of Land Management
Burns District Office
HC 74–12533 Highway 20 West
Hines, OR 97738
(541) 573–4400
www.or.blm.gov

Borax Lake and Borax Hot Springs
The Nature Conservancy of Oregon
821 Southeast Fourteenth Avenue
Portland, OR 97214
(503) 230–1221
nature.org/wherewework/northamerica/
states/oregon/preserves/art6794.html

Crystal Crane Hot Springs
HC 73–2653 Highway 78
Burns, OR 97720
(541) 493–2312
www.crystalcranehotsprings.com

Mickey Hot Springs
Bureau of Land Management
Burns District Office
HC 74–12533 Highway 20 West
Hines, OR 97738
(541) 573–4400
www.or.blm.gov

Willow Creek (Whitehorse Ranch)
Hot Springs
Bureau of Land Management
Burns District Office
HC 74–12533 Highway 20 West
Hines, OR 97738
(541) 573–4400
www.or.blm.gov

Resources

Geo-Heat Center
Oregon Institute of Technology
3201 Campus Drive
Klamath Falls, OR 97601
(541) 885–1750
www.geoheat.oit.edu

The Geo-Heat Center provides technical assistance to individuals and companies involved in geothermal-energy development. The center also hosts a library of more than 5,000 books and maps on geothermal energy and hot springs, as well as an on-line database of information on almost 9,000 thermal springs and wells in the western United States.

Litton, Evie. *Hiking Hot Springs in the Pacific Northwest,* 3d ed. Guilford, Conn.: The Globe Pequot Press, 2001.
www.globe-pequot.com

Litton's popular hot springs guide focuses on undeveloped backcountry soaks. Included are several Oregon and Washington hot springs, as well as descriptions of nearby hikes.

The Hot Springs Gazette
240 North Jones Suite 161
Las Vegas, NV 89107
www.hotspringsgazette.com

This quarterly publication features articles and photos of mostly undeveloped hot springs in the western United States. The Hot Springs Gazette has been in publication for more than twenty years and has a loyal following.

Northwest Natural Hot Springs Discussion Board
www.nwhotsprings.net

This discussion board overlaps with Soak.net; you'll often find the same messages posted to both Web sites. Northwest Natural Hot Springs focuses exclusively on hot springs of the Pacific Northwest.

Soak.net—A Place for Natural Hot Springs Resources
www.soak.net

Soak.net is perhaps the best on-line discussion board for finding current conditions at undeveloped hot springs in the western United States. The emphasis is definitely on noncommercial soaks, although occasionally there is some mention of commercial resorts.

Index

References to maps are printed in boldface type.

Delta Campground, 78
Depot Park, 133
Devine, John, 189
Doan, Robert, 183–84
Doe Bay Café, 31
Doe Bay Village Resort, 11–12, 27–32,
  28
Douglas, John, 133

E
Earles, Michael, 17–19
Eugene, Oregon, 66–91
Everett, William, 24

F
Fields, Oregon, 179–85
Frazier Campground, 143
Freeman, Terry, 120
Frémont, John C., 113–14
French Pete Campground, 78
Fulton, John M., 184–85

G
Geyser (Hunter's) Hot Springs Resort,
  116–20, **117**
Glacier Peak Wilderness, 9
Goldfish Lake, 118
Goldmyer Hot Springs, 9
Graham, Duane, 115
Grand Coulee Dam, 49
Grande Ronde Valley, 145–58

H
Hardin, John, 90–91
Hart Mountain National Antelope
  Refuge, 121–25
Hawk, John, 73
Hegewald, Rudy, 43
Helman Baths, 100
Homestead Campground, 78
Hot Lake Hotel and Sanitarium, 2, 11,
  145–51, **146**
Hot Lake RV Resort, 152–54, **153**
hot springs
  behaving responsibly at, 7–8

best for families, 11
best nude soak, 11–12
changing situations at, 4
checklist for visits to, 6–7
history of, 1–3
most eclectic, 12
most historic, 11
most remote, 10
most romantic, 12
safety precautions for, 5–6
using topographical maps to locate,
  4–5
Hot Springs Campground, 123
Hudson's Bay Company, 47, 120
Humbug Campground, 61
Hunter, Harry, 120
Hunter's Chlorine Hot Springs Club,
  120

I
Iland, Minne, 166–67
Irving, Washington, 2, 147

J
Jackson, Eugenia, 100
Jackson Hot Springs, 99
Jacobs, A. J., 79
Jacobsen, Andrew, 24

K
Kah-Nee-Ta Resort, 11, 105–10, **106**
Kaufman, Charles R., 134–35
Kennedy Hot Springs, 9
Kingfisher Campground, 55
Kingsbury Springs, 100
Kryger, Dan and Denise, 167

L
La Grande, Oregon, 141–63
Lahontan cutthroat trout, 190
Lakeview, Oregon, 111–25
Lasater, Shorty, 167
Lehman, James, 143, 144
Lehman Hot Springs, 141–44, **142**
Lehrburger, Gerry, 99

About the Author

Jeff Birkby's fascination with hot springs began in the early 1980s, when he managed geothermal-energy projects for the Montana Department of Natural Resources. During his years of geothermal-energy consulting, Jeff developed a passion for hot-springs lore, especially the stories and legends of hot springs of the northwestern United States. In 1999 Jeff authored the FalconGuide *Touring Montana and Wyoming Hot Springs*.

When he's not soaking in the natural hot-water pools of the American West, Jeff manages renewable-energy programs for the nonprofit National Center for Appropriate Technology in Butte, Montana.

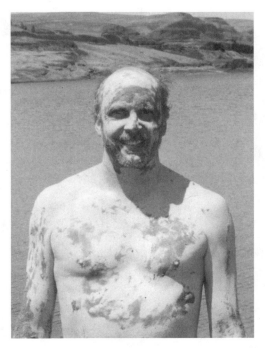

Author Jeff Birkby samples the rejuvenating mud of Soap Lake, Washington.